growing
local value

THE SOCIAL VENTURE NETWORK SERIES

growing local value

HOW TO BUILD BUSINESS PARTNERSHIPS
THAT STRENGTHEN YOUR COMMUNITY

Laury Hammel
Gun Denhart

BERRETT-KOEHLER PUBLISHERS, INC.
San Francisco

Berrett-Koehler Publishers, Inc.
235 Montgomery Street, Suite 650
San Francisco, CA 94104-2916
Tel: (415) 288-0260   Fax: (415) 362-2512   www.bkconnection.com

Ordering Information
Quantity sales. Special discounts are available on quantity purchases by corporations, associations, and others. For details, contact the "Special Sales Department" at the Berrett-Koehler address above.
Individual sales. Berrett-Koehler publications are available through most bookstores. They can also be ordered directly from Berrett-Koehler: Tel: (800) 929-2929; Fax: (802) 864-7626; http://www.bkconnection.com.
Orders for college textbook/course adoption use. Please contact Berrett-Koehler: Tel: (800) 929-2929; Fax: (802) 864-7626.
Orders by U.S. trade bookstores and wholesalers. Please contact Publishers Group West, 1700 Fourth Street, Berkeley, CA 94710. Tel: (510) 528-1444; Fax (510) 528-3444.

Berrett-Koehler and the BK logo are registered trademarks of Berrett-Koehler Publishers, Inc.

Printed in the United States of America

Berrett-Koehler books are printed on long-lasting acid-free paper.

Library of Congress Cataloging-in-Publication Data
Hammel, Laury.
    Growing local value : how to build business partnerships that
strengthen your community / by Laury Hammel and Gun Denhart.
    p. cm. — (The social venture network series)
    Includes bibliographical references.
    ISBN-13: 978-1-57675-371-2 (pbk.)
    1. Social responsibility of business—United States—Case studies. 2. Industries—Social aspects—United States—Case studies. 3. Community leadership—United States—Case studies. 4. Civic improvement—United States—Case studies. 5. Public-private sector cooperation—United States—Case studies. I. Denhart, Gun. II. Title. III. Title: Business partnerships that strengthen your community.
HD60.5.U5H354   2007
658.4'08—dc22   2006031101

FIRST EDITION
11 10 09 08 07 06   10 9 8 7 6 5 4 3 2 1

	ENVIRONMENTAL BENEFITS STATEMENT			
	For every 5,000 books printed, **Berrett-Koehler Publishers** saved the following resources by using New Leaf EcoBook 50, made with 100%			
NEW LEAF PAPER™	recycled fiber and 50% post-consumer waste, processed chlorine free.			
trees	water	energy	solid waste	greenhouse gases
22 fully grown	**7,607** gallons	**14** million Btu	**992** pounds	**1,701** pounds
Calculations based on research by Environmental Defense and other members of the Paper Task Force.				
©2006 New Leaf Paper www.newleafpaper.com				

*To my father and mother, Lee and Ruby Hammel,
who taught me to love life and serve God. To my
children, Sara, Jed, Eliza, Jason, and Samantha, who
inspire me every day. And to Myke and Jo Ellen Farricker,
my business partners of twenty-five years. Jo Ellen left
us way too soon, and we miss her spirit encouraging us to
change the world one person at a time.*

— LAURY

*To my father, who taught me about
business, my mother, who taught
me about service, and my husband,
who supported me.*

— GUN

Contents

Letter from the Editor of the Social Venture Network Series

Let me guess. You probably picked up this book because you're looking for innovative ways that your business can become more engaged in the community (or communities) where you do business. And that's exactly what you'll find in these pages.

Gun Denhart and Laury Hammel are two of the most creative and committed entrepreneurs in Social Venture Network. Their dedication to enriching the lives of those who work and live around them, their flair for innovation, and their business savvy come through clearly in *Growing Local Value*. They've drawn on dozens of outstanding examples of community-minded companies—including their own—to provide you with a treasure-house of ideas you can put to work to make your own business more responsive to community needs, more rewarding for everyone who works for you—and more competitive as a result.

If you are laboring under the conventional wisdom that the only responsibility of a business is to its owners or shareholders, you'll find that view demolished in this slim volume (as in every other book in the Social Venture Network series). This is the paradox of socially responsible business: the more successfully you respond to the needs of all your stakeholders—employees, customers, suppliers, community members, and the environment as well as the people who put up the money and take most of the financial risks—the more likely it is that your company will thrive. What goes around, comes around. You'll see this time and again in the inspiring examples cited by Laury Hammel and Gun Denhart in this invaluable little handbook.

In this book, we discuss a new way to run a company—using humane values as the driving force of the business. We see ourselves as part of a broader movement to transform commerce from a system that is destructive of our earth and economically unjust to one that is sustainable and fair. However, the word *local* in our title has significance all its own.

Science has helped surround us with great conveniences and connect us electronically with people everywhere. But these advances come at a high price. Our experiences are filtered through electronic devices—television, cell phones, and the Internet—and we lack direct contact with real people. These "mediated experiences" have created in many of us a great yearning to touch and connect more deeply and naturally with other people.

Personal relationships develop more easily and often grow deeper when we participate in activities in our local community. Activities such as shopping, participating in school and civic events, and working out all take on greater meaning in today's world. Human beings are social animals, and a desire to be with people is embedded within our DNA. This longing for human contact is central to our physical, mental, and spiritual health. We all want to be a part of a community and to feel connected with a sense of place.

People intuitively understand the value of doing business with people they know and trust. We appreciate our relationship with the owner of the local hardware store. We long to restore our relationship with the local pharmacist who couldn't compete with the chains and was forced to close shop. Buying locally also helps build strong local economies. Economic studies in Texas, Maine, and Illinois have shown that when a customer purchases a product from a locally owned business, more money stays in the community. The most recent of these studies, conducted in Andersonville, Illinois, in October 2004, evaluated the economic role played by independent businesses. The results showed that for every $100 in consumer spending with a local firm, $68 remains in the Chicago economy versus $43 for spending at a chain store.[1] The economic multiplier (which indicates the economic impact and ripple effect of purchasing from local businesses) increases with each new local purchase.[2] A strong retail district of locally owned businesses also builds unique and interesting places for residents to gather and have fellowship. Shopping locally just makes sense.

By partnering with all the various stakeholders in your business—customers, employees, vendors, fellow businesses, owners/investors, nonprofits, the environment, and the public sector—you can grow local value. All of these stakeholders make up your community, which in this book means everyone and everything that resides in a small geographic area, usually a town or city. If your business is located in more than one town or city, your local community may include all these stakeholders at every location.

Leading entrepreneurs seek to balance the needs of all stakeholders in the community. The term *stakeholder* represents an important concept in the language of business because it acknowledges that a company does not operate in isolation and is, in fact, dependent on many constituencies for its success. Furthermore, these partners all have a stake in the business, and their interests need to be considered when management decisions are made. Another way of simplifying this concept is to use the term *triple bottom line,* which some entrepreneurs use to describe their business mission—to support people, the planet, and profits.

In this book you'll read how values-driven entrepreneurs all across America have successfully created partnerships where everyone involved wins—the entrepreneur and all the stakeholders. In fact, as will become abundantly clear to you as you make your way through these pages, we believe that building partnerships in the community will help you gain a competitive advantage that will allow you to compete more effectively and build a stronger business.

In each of the following seven chapters, we'll focus on one of the seven key stakeholder groups. Each chapter will show how you can build bridges leading to meaningful partnerships with that stakeholder group. We'll relate an exceptional example of a values-driven business that has successfully leveraged its strength to grow local value. Of course, we all make mistakes. Painful management decisions often set the stage for future good decisions, resulting in a more experienced and intelligent management team, so the entrepreneurs from each company will share a management mistake they made. You'll also learn how the company struggles with a challenging and ongoing "management tension." You know as well as we do that running a business can get messy, and dealing with the conflicting needs of stakeholders can be challenging. Next you'll read a sampling of best practices used by other companies to create innovative and replicable partnerships that represent a wide range of industries.

Finally, each chapter will conclude with a series of lessons. Our hope is that this book will not only inspire you to find new ways to generate revenue but save you time and money by helping you learn from the mistakes and successes of some of North America's leading entrepreneurs.

Much of our business success has come from learning from the experience of others and finding ways to innovate and add value to our products and our communities.

Gun Denhart is the founder of Hanna Andersson, a $95 million clothing retail business, known to customers throughout North America for durable children's clothing that lets kids be kids. In its hometown of Portland, Oregon, Hanna is recognized as a good corporate citizen, supporting programs and initiatives that put children first. Hanna has set up a foundation that supports vulnerable children in communities where the company operates.

Laury Hammel founded the Longfellow Clubs in 1980, starting with one tennis club outside Boston. The Longfellow Clubs is now a group of health and sports clubs, holistic health centers, and children's centers and camps with $15 million in revenues. Longfellow serves twelve thousand members and is the fourth largest independent health club business in New England. The Longfellow Clubs' mission is to enhance the health and well-being of all people in the community. Its programs include tennis classes for people with special needs, alcohol-free overnight prom parties, and discounted memberships for local town employees.

We've loved the journey of entrepreneurship, and we feel blessed to have had the opportunity to pour ourselves into worthy missions. We have forged meaningful partnerships between our businesses and our communities. And we've learned that the stronger that bond, the more the partners benefit.

We've both intentionally surrounded ourselves with staff members who share our deep commitment to the missions of our companies. Our teams' enthusiasm enables us to overcome obstacles and ultimately produce what many view as extraordinary results.

Like all entrepreneurs, we've made critical choices along the path of building our companies. Some ideas worked and some didn't. For better or for worse, each management decision had to meet the standards and values of our companies and our personal consciences. We know that thousands of small and large decisions cumulatively determine the integrity of an entrepreneur and the soul of a business. And from a practical perspective, we really had no choice. It was either do what our hearts were telling us to do or be miserable.

We've met hundreds of entrepreneurs who share our desire to do well while doing good. Like us, they are hungry to both grow their businesses *and* better serve the needs of their communities. But these entrepreneurs tend to be overworked, underfinanced, and often overwhelmed with making payroll or dealing with the inevitable daily crises that arise.

This book offers a road map with a variety of possible routes toward growing local value. Each path will help you move your business in the direction you choose. Every entrepreneurial passion is different, and each business is unique. Our aim is to encourage you to create strategies that will transform a worthy vision into a healthy living reality. Please use and abuse this book. Underline it, highlight it, write notes, e-mail excerpts, pass it around the office—whatever works to stimulate conversation within your business.

1

Customer and community first

An entrepreneur finds a need and fills it. However, if you're one of a fast-growing group of people starting and running companies all across the country (and that includes us), you want to build a business that goes a step further and fills real needs that will improve the quality of people's lives.

Unfortunately, not all successful businesses sell products that make our lives better. A consumerist culture driven by omnipresent marketing often influences us to buy things we really don't need. When products are designed to meet artificial needs, they generally have a negative impact on our communities.

Of course, determining which needs are real and which are not can be tricky. You may be thinking that no one should pretend to determine your real needs. And you might even ask, "Shouldn't the marketplace alone determine whether or not a product succeeds?" Yes, the marketplace is the absolute ruler when it comes to the success or failure of a product.

But it's also true that in most cases, long-term business success is directly related to the ultimate value of the product to society. We're sure you could point out plenty of examples of products that have been around for a long time that don't serve real needs, but as a rule, the products with the longest staying power tend to be the ones that meet actual needs. And going a step further, plenty of us are looking to make purchases that offer genuine value and also match our values. Whether we're considering a hybrid car or Seventh Generation paper towels, we've definitely become more discriminating customers.

The desire to meet a real need has probably been the driving force motivating you to start your own business. We are passionate about supporting emerging entrepreneurs, and it's exciting for us to know that hundreds of thousands of needs remain to be met in communities all over the world. And these needs offer tremendous opportunities for would-be entrepreneurs to start businesses that make tangible contributions to their communities.

Most likely, you understand intuitively the importance of community relations. You may already be partnering with your customers to improve community life (or planning to do so). For example, whereas many people view purchasing a plant at a local garden center as a simple and uncomplicated transaction, you may, as we do, view it as one episode in an ongoing partnership that will last as long as you live in your community. If you follow this logic a step further, you'll see that when an entrepreneur works to develop deep and lasting partnerships with customers, both the community and the business receive a multitude of benefits.

Of course, building partnerships with customers requires that you do more than merely offer a product to meet a one-time need. When you forge vibrant business-customer partnerships, you are deeply connected to the customers and you learn the depth and breadth of a particular category of needs. You find yourself naturally working hand in hand with customers and continually searching for new and better ways to meet their needs. By actively nurturing these relationships, engaging in meaningful conversations with customers, and never taking these pivotal relationships for granted, you work yourself into the hearts of the customers and the community. Those strong partnerships with your customers will then become a major competitive advantage for your business. Conversely, complacency regarding customer relationships is deadly: customers are fluid, their needs change, and new competitors are always springing up, ready to take your place.

You may have observed that when customers rave about how much they love doing business with a company, developing partnerships with them as a way of contributing to the community follows naturally. These dynamic partnerships can take a variety of forms, including

- Creating a quality product that fulfills a real community need and is consistently upgraded and customized in response to feedback from customers
- Collaborating with customers to support charities, local nonprofits, or community events, such as Earth Day celebrations
- Partnering with customers to improve community life by supporting government agencies and schools
- Finding ways to expand your customer base to include people who may not be able to afford your product at the standard prices
- Reaching out to populations in your community who would like to use your product but do not have access to it because of distance, inability to travel, or personal schedule

In this chapter, we'll describe the experiences of four companies—the Longfellow Clubs, TAGS Hardware, the King's English Book Shop, and Joie de Vivre Hospitality—to illustrate how businesses can partner with customers to grow local value.

Partnering with Customers:
The Longfellow Clubs, Wayland, Massachusetts

In 1980 Laury Hammel founded a business that has embraced the guiding principles of this book from day one. Beginning as one tennis-only club outside Boston, the Longfellow Clubs has grown into a group of health and sports clubs, holistic health centers, and children's centers and camps. Longfellow has become a recognized industry leader in innovative business practices, social responsibility, and community service.

While at the University of Utah in the sixties, Laury was a civil-rights, antiwar, and environmental activist. Laury's story is that of an entrepreneur who built a business by creating innovative products that met real community needs. He rejected the prevailing way of doing business—making the single bottom line of profits paramount. Instead, he valued the relationships with all stakeholders and measured success by tracking multiple bottom lines.

Laury's desire to meet the needs of his customers pushed him into starting the business in the first place. If someone had told him in the sixties that he would one day be a businessman, he would have laughed at the absurdity or wept at what he perceived as "selling out to the establishment." Having played competitive tennis since the age of ten, he fell into teaching tennis. This was at the height of the tennis boom, and millions of people were lining up to learn this rapidly growing sport.

Laury found himself in the right place at the right time, and he utilized his playing and teaching skills to create a highly successful tennis program. In the process, he unwittingly became a businessman, an "intrapreneur" working inside clubs owned by others. He didn't see this as running a business. He did what he loved and saw himself simply as making tennis fun for people of all ages, genders, and incomes and training and organizing other tennis pros to do the same. His initial experience was with club owners who had adversarial relationships with their members. As Laury became more involved in the club business, it began to dawn on him that maybe a business could be managed in a way that authentically cared about the customers and was still profitable.

This insight led him and his partner Myke Farricker to open their first club in 1980. Laury, Myke, and their management team immediately began looking for ways to run their business differently—to manage it with values in the forefront. One of their first actions was to take the then highly unusual step of crafting their mission statement:

> To build a world where people's basic needs are met and people experience love, happiness, and satisfaction.

> To run a tennis and recreation business that works toward the fulfillment of our global vision.

For more than twenty-five years since those words were written, a successful community-based business has flowed from the wellspring of these shared values.

Throughout Laury's life, he had always placed a premium on relationships. He found that the best way to develop strong and lasting relationships was to listen to people and respond with care. When he entered the world of business, he addressed the expressed and observed needs of his clients by inventing new ways to teach tennis and run programs. His passion for excellence on and off the court and his capacity for listening to his clients resulted in large numbers of what author Ken Blanchard calls "Raving Fans." Laury knew that it wasn't good enough to have satisfied customers; he wanted customers who were blown away by the results.

Laury created a company culture that focused on customers and how his business could meet the needs of the community. This perspective gradually grew into a series of partnerships with club members. These partnerships began with straight-forward efforts such as building a strong women's team and teaching participants how to improve their game and have more fun and eventually included a low-cost tennis program for young people with special needs. The deeper these relationships grew, the more opportunities for customer partnerships arose. It wasn't long before Longfellow expanded to meet the health and fitness needs of the community by offering facilities and programs for strength training, group exercise, cardio fitness, basketball, swimming, and water exercise, to name a few. As the clubs continued to evolve, Longfellow opened children's centers and holistic health centers offering healing modalities such as chiropractic, acupuncture, massage therapy, and physical therapy.

Laury and his staff have learned that when connections with their customers are strong, partnerships to improve the community happen naturally. Their efforts now include

- Partnering with customers to participate in community events to support nonprofit organizations and schools
- Adopting a policy of saying yes to all requests by members for in-kind (product) and/or cash donations to local community groups or events
- Teaming with members to raise money for a local charity race, walk, or health fair

Through efforts such as these, Longfellow has become a platform for community residents to work together to help make a more livable and healthy community.

An Idea Whose Time Had Not Come

Not all of Longfellow's initiatives have been successful. For example, once Laury had an "outside-the-box" idea to open a restaurant in his second club.

One of the key ingredients for success in starting a business is having passion for the product. But sometimes that passion can blind us to the lack of demand from customers and other reasons to abandon or modify a new product.

This was the case with Laury in 1986. He had just opened his second multipurpose club, and it had a perfect spot for a full-service restaurant (overlooking two new basketball courts). In his mind's eye, he could see patrons enjoying good, healthy food and a glass of beer or wine while watching high-level basketball through the floor-to-ceiling windows. No restaurant within miles specialized in natural and organic vegetarian cuisine, so Laury believed the restaurant would fill a need. He was convinced this new venture would complement Longfellow's emphasis on health and fitness.

He hired a restaurant manager and designed and built a full-service restaurant and complete kitchen. Unfortunately, on opening day, no one but staff and a few close friends came to eat. Perhaps, he thought, it would take a few days for the word to get out. However, days turned into weeks and weeks into months, and still no one was eating there but a few staff members. Longfellow changed the menu and added meat. It lowered the prices, but the place was still empty. And every day, cash was flowing out and none was coming in. After losing over $300,000, Laury was forced to shut down the restaurant and make it a function room.

Twenty years later, Laury realizes he broke many rules and ignored several facts. First, few if any health clubs in the nation have profitable restaurants. Second, nonmembers generally won't go into a club they don't belong to, and members alone can't support a restaurant. And, third, the reason why the area had no vegetarian restaurants was there simply wasn't enough demand.

The restaurant may have been a wonderful idea, but it was an idea whose time had not come. Laury was convinced his new venture filled a real need, but his potential customers didn't see it that way. He was a willing partner in this venture, but precious few customers shared his enthusiasm. A one-way partnership never works. Laury learned the hard way that the marketplace can be an accurate, if brutal, indicator of what customers are willing to purchase.

Balancing Pricing for Profit with Reaching a Broader Customer Base

At its birth, Longfellow was committed to offering its services to people of all ages, genders, abilities, and incomes. But could this be done while still making a profit? How Laury and his team handled this management tension offers lessons for us all.

The mission of Longfellow is to make the world a better place, and a logical extension would be to price Longfellow's products so that all people could afford them. However, multipurpose health clubs require constant capital improvements and new equipment, and payroll expenses are high. Consequently, the prices required to ensure profitability often push some potential customers out of the market.

This creates a contradiction: Longfellow's purpose is to provide services that support all people's health, and yet its typical prices exclude many middle- and low-income people. What did Longfellow do to mitigate this management tension? The first step was to acknowledge that it was an ongoing issue that needed to be addressed by management. The next step was to brainstorm about how to deal with this tension. Laury and his management team developed a policy to make every effort to never turn a person away, and they found numerous ways to make the clubs' services available, including

- Hiring highly skilled part-time staff members to work a few hours a week so they can have full use of all the facilities.
- Partnering with local towns to put together special programs for schoolteachers and police and fire department employees. The individuals, the towns, and Longfellow all contribute to the membership fees.
- Working closely with a local HMO (health maintenance organization) to provide full membership at a reduced rate. In addition, seniors and juniors are welcomed with a price reduction of 20 percent.
- Offering unemployed people or those who are in a personal crisis and struggling financially complimentary or steeply discounted memberships to help them build their strength while they get back on their feet.
- Pricing off-peak court time at a very affordable fee.
- Seeking out talented young tennis players who may not be able to pay for a complete program and giving them scholarships.

Many members are aware of these policies and regularly step forward with a person or family in need.

Having done all of this, Laury still wasn't satisfied. His clubs are located in wealthy communities where most of the residents are Caucasian. Because most people will travel no more than twenty minutes each way to a health club, Longfellow's locations limit the diversity of its customer base. Laury considered opening clubs in lower-income neighborhoods. However, the core business involves tennis, which requires substantial land, and no location in the city of Boston was financially viable.

In the late nineties, Longfellow took an important step in resolving this management tension. Laury had a long-standing relationship with the Sportsmen's Tennis Club, a Boston inner-city indoor/outdoor tennis club founded by African Americans. In 1997 it was on the verge of closing its doors. Laury and Longfellow were asked to step in and manage the club. Laury signed a management contract for one dollar a year, and he soon found himself traveling forty-five minutes to the Dorchester neighborhood two to three times a week to help rebuild this important community institution.

By the end of 2002—when the club had recovered and the formal management contract had ended—Longfellow had made an enormous impact. Under the new management, enrollment in the free children's programs grew from 43 to over 500, and the summer camp grew from 40 children a week to over 130. The worn-out courts were resurfaced, four new state-of-the-art outdoor courts were built, the dim lighting was replaced and upgraded, the leaky roof was fixed, the offices and lobby were remodeled, and the outside of the building was painted. The tennis professionals' pay was increased, and staff training programs were put in place. Sportsmen's was experiencing a rebirth. During these five years, Laury and Longfellow raised over $1,000,000, donated over $75,000 in cash, provided over $400,000 in in-kind services, and loaned the club over $100,000.

This partnership stands as an excellent example of a business expanding its customer base. Even though it didn't bring in any revenue, it served Longfellow's social mission and generated immense amounts of goodwill.

Best Practices in Partnering with Customers

Just as Laury Hammel has built a thriving business grounded in his commitment to serving his customers and the larger community of which they're a part, so has Simon Shapiro. Simon, proprietor of TAGS Hardware, has an old-fashioned ethic of partnering with customers by taking care of them both as patrons of his business and as residents of the community they share.

Take Care of Your Customer and Your Community: TAGS Hardware, Cambridge, Massachusetts

In many communities, locally owned hardware stores have gone the way of the horse and buggy. Every time a big-box home improvement store pops up, small businesses nearby suffer or, worse, just disappear. Fortunately, Cambridge, Massachusetts, still has a number of small local hardware stores that are thriving.

After spending many years in retail, Simon Shapiro began working at TAGS Hardware in Cambridge, Massachusetts, in 1972 when it was grossing around $170,000 in revenues. By 1982 he was running the family business. A year later he met his future wife, Margaret (Mardi) Moran, and by 1986 she became involved in the business. Today this husband-wife team manages TAGS. Simon serves as the CEO, and Mardie is the president of this beloved community institution that has 25,000 square feet of retail space and generates almost $7 million in revenues.

Originally in the movie theater business, Simon's father, Norton Shapiro, founded TAGS in 1955 with the help of a relative who was having great success in the hardware store business. In response to customer needs, the store grew over the years to be more of a small department store, stocking items including hammers, small kitchen appliances, and garden supplies.

How does TAGS compete with the big-box stores? According to Simon, TAG's success and longevity are directly related to the business mantra drilled into him by his father: "Take care of the customer, and the customer will take care of you." This fundamental value permeates everything TAGS does, and the company is on a continual search to find new ways to meet customers' needs.

The most important way that TAGS serves customers is with superior service provided by highly trained staff. Every new staff member goes through a standard orientation and receives constant on-the-floor training. Regular off-the-floor educational meetings focus on new products and are led by in-house and outside experts. Opportunities for staff to hear the customers' perspective include regular reports from professional "secret shoppers." Creating a pleasant shopping experience and providing exemplary service by answering customers' questions, locating requested items, and finding solutions to problems is the mission of every TAGS employee.

TAGS employees work as a team. They meet every morning and go over sales goals, new products, and special offers and programs. During the day, department managers help out when needed. And TAGS doesn't skimp on staffing. Every department keeps at least one staff member easily visible to customers.

TAGS is famous for the innovative ways it partners with customers. For example, every new Cambridge resident gets a coupon in the mail offering a free trash can and a duplicate house key. TAGS also sends out "free light bulb cards" to frequent customers. TAGS gives away an average of 650 light bulbs every month. The high point of the year's calendar is TAGS's Customer Appreciation Weekend in November. This wonderful extravaganza includes Mr. and Mrs. Santa Claus, product demonstrations offering taste treats, free popcorn, and fun activities.

TAGS is located in Porter Square on busy Massachusetts Avenue within walking distance of a subway stop. Yet some local residents still drive a significant distance to compare prices at big-box stores. TAGS carefully studies the competition to ensure TAGS merchandise is priced competitively.

Simon's business ethic stems from his father's deeply held values. Not only did Norton Shapiro preach taking care of customers, he said it was the responsibility of a business to give back to the community. Nonprofit organizations in Cambridge know they can count on TAGS as a partner. Whether it's paint and brushes or a hammer and nails, every reasonable request is honored and no one goes away empty-handed.

TAGS's return policy also reflects a deep commitment to the community. TAGS will take back any merchandise within thirty days of purchase, and returned items in good condition are promptly given to worthy nonprofits in the community, including a local agency that helps battered women get a new, independent start in life.

It's not surprising that Simon and Mardie are very involved in community affairs. A Cambridge resident for over twenty-five years, Simon spends a lot of time partnering with various community groups, whether it's building up the infrastructure of the Porter Square business district, regularly representing the business community in City of Cambridge issues, or promoting the growth of Cambridge Local First, an organization of locally owned independent businesses that promotes local businesses.

When asked why he doesn't open other TAGS stores, he replied, "Because I don't want to fail. I wouldn't know how to service a suburban crowd; I have no idea how to sell a power lawn mower." We suspect that Simon could learn to sell a power lawn mower but that he sees his consistent presence at TAGS and his deep relationships with customers and staff to be mandatory for success—and his pleasure.

Like Simon, Betsy Burton is in retail, and she's also a respected community leader in her hometown of Salt Lake City, Utah. *Partnership* and *collaboration* are two words that describe the very essence of Betsy, her entrepreneurship, and her community leadership. In a city that tends to be divided by religion and culture, Betsy is a bridge builder, and her business and her community are the better for it.

Personalizing Your Product:
The King's English Book Shop, Salt Lake City, Utah

Betsy Burton has taken the concept of being close to the customer to a glorious level of intimacy. The King's English Book Shop has found fun and deeply meaningful ways to touch the souls of its customers. Meeting practical needs isn't the goal here—Betsy's work is all about the heart, the emotions, the invisible parts of us that have a yearning. Be it a thirst for knowledge, a desire for romance, or the healing of an open wound, Betsy, her staff, and her many author friends offer care and an open ear. Nothing brings her more satisfaction and joy than successfully building a bridge from a customer to a good book!

"Contortionists one and all, we [independent booksellers] delight in climbing into other people's skins or clothes or shoes in order to walk a mile or two along another's path. We question them and listen carefully to the replies, intent on deciphering what they want. The real pleasure in bookselling comes in pairing the right book with the right person. That's what drives us as we look, listen, assess, ask questions until—bingo!—we come up with a match."[3]

And it must be a match from the customer's point of view. Betsy aims to give customers what they want, not what she thinks they should want. When this happens, she's found it can change lives.

The inspiration for the King's English Book Shop came about during conversations between Betsy and her good friend, Ann Berman, about what their own bookstore might look like. The more they talked, the more excited they became about their concept, and before long they found themselves opening the doors of their new business.

In the early days, they would talk with customers forty to sixty hours a week, take boxes home and unpack them, check packing lists, haul everything back to the store, and pay bills. And after doing all the work necessary to keep the business moving forward, they'd stay up nights reading every book they could.

A bench where customers would sit and talk with Betsy or Ann became known as the confessional bench. Here people would share their tales of tough divorces and betrayals, deaths, and other deep sorrows. Betsy and Ann recommended books that soothed people's souls and helped create customers for life.

Very early on, Betsy saw the importance of working in the community to promote good literature and, in particular, to introduce new authors to her customers. She believed that she could generate enthusiasm for books by partnering with customers on a variety of community events. To that end, Betsy has hosted public presentations and book signings featuring famous and not-so-famous authors. Other community activities that represent partnerships with customers to enliven the community include

- Creating the Writers Advocacy Award for those promoting literacy in the community
- Partnering with Westminster College in a three-day symposium featuring a prominent poet or fiction writer
- Supporting a University of Utah science and literature series to open up an interdisciplinary conversation
- Organizing a wide variety of book clubs for adults
- Serving on the Salt Lake City Book Club Committee, which encourages people to join book clubs and runs an annual book festival
- Supporting the books behind bars literacy program (run by a nonprofit organization founded by a local judge) for inmates in the city jail

Many neighborhood children stop by the store after school because it's a safe place to spend time and read. Betsy knows that the future of books resides with the children, so she brings in popular authors such as Lemony Snickett to encourage them to experience the magic and wonder of books. The King's English does much to encourage children to read, including

- Offering a Children's Story Hour every week
- Organizing Kids Reading Clubs complete with games and prizes
- Hosting nights at the bookshop for teachers and librarians, giving them discounts and handing out possible curricula for classes

The King's English has become much more than a place to pick up a book. It is an empowering community resource as well as a community within a community. The feeling of connection and partnership that customers have has enabled Betsy and her small independent bookstore to thrive in an industry that is dominated by big-box stores and online sellers.

Betsy also understands that her business success isn't strictly about growing market share in the face of intense competition. It's about creating more customers for literature. For this reason she has immersed herself in the bookselling industry both nationally and locally. As a result, all the leading independent Utah bookstores now work as partners to bring authors to the area, trade books, and offer mutual support.

Betsy Burton builds friendships and partnerships that form the foundation of her single-location business and simultaneously grow local value. Can such personalized service and deep connections happen in several locations? Chip Conley has created a model for how powerful business-customer partnerships can thrive in a multiple-location business.

Connecting Customers with the Community:
Joie de Vivre Hospitality, San Francisco, California

Joie de Vivre Hospitality (JDV), founded by Chip Conley in 1987, operates thirty boutique hotels (with 3,200 rooms), eight restaurants, and three day spas located primarily in the San Francisco Bay Area. Chip's business not only grosses over $100 million annually, but it actually lives up to its name, which means "joy of life." The staff-authored mission statement, "Creating opportunities to celebrate the joy of life," is the holy grail of JDV, and everything the company does focuses on personalizing this celebration.

Chip's hotels are designed with great flair, and each one is styled after a particular magazine. JDV's most famous hotel, the Phoenix, has décor, services, amenities, and an overall identity influenced by *Rolling Stone* magazine. Rather than focusing on demographics, the company's marketing emphasizes "psychographics," with each property appealing to a different taste. JDV has even gone so far as to introduce Yvette, the online Hotel Matchmaker, as a way of helping guests find the perfect hotel to fit their personality. Guests are asked to fill out a short personality test that gives Yvette an idea of which hotel they might like. She also suggests six cool local activities that fit each guest's personality profile. Her work has been well received by customers, and Yvette has become a bit of an icon.

While most hotels aim to provide a good night's sleep, JDV is more concerned with creating wonderful dreams. Chip's vision is to develop deep and lasting relationships with his customers and to transcend simply providing a service to his guests. JDV fosters vibrant partnerships that bring joy to customers by honoring their diversity and individuality and enabling them to transform their dreams into reality. JDV hotels reject sameness and homogeneous branding and instead embrace a distinctive character and offer a tangibly different experience. This commitment to establishing a dynamic difference in product reflects the company's respect for the uniqueness of each customer. And the proof that these are real partnerships is in the pudding of repeat customers.

Besides helping rekindle the tourism industry in the Bay Area, JDV hotels also strive to educate their guests about hidden treasures and off-the-beaten-path places that make San Francisco so special. They play an important role in steering dollars into the local economy by promoting local and independent businesses and nonprofits.

JDV also grows local value through customer partnerships in many ways that go beyond uplifting the lives of guests. In 1996 it opened the Hotel Rex, which has a theme of arts and literature. At the time, Congress was involved in a big ruckus about censoring art and cutting federal funding for the National Endowment for the Arts (NEA). Although the NEA survived, severe federal funding cutbacks were instituted. As a way to support the arts, the Rex offered all guests a list of thirteen local arts organizations to which they could contribute $5 of the price for each night's stay. Customers and JDV together raised over $40,000!

Another JDV hotel, the Carlton Hotel, has recently partnered with the Kohala Foundation, a charitable organization founded by SVN member David Levenson. Kohala's "Win a Week with Us" is a donation program for hotel customers. Every Thanksgiving a drawing is held for all donors and the winner receives a free week's stay at the Carlton. When guests register for a room, they are asked if they'd like to round up their bill and contribute the extra amount to the Raphael House (located next door to the hotel), which helps feed homeless people and offers them job training programs. As of this writing, the Carlton is averaging $12 per donation and has a 9 percent visi-

tor participation level. Over $1,000 per month in customer do-
nations is going to the Raphael House. Guests appreciate the opportunity to support a local nonprofit, and this psychic bridge
connects them more deeply with the local community.

Lessons Learned: Partnering with Customers

Maybe the business you're running (or the one you want to start)
isn't a health club, a hardware store, a bookshop, or a hotel
chain. But the experiences of these four world-class small businesses have a lot to teach us, no matter what industry we're in.
Following are just a few of the many lessons you might take
away from the examples we've cited in this chapter:

- **Listen, listen, listen.** The closer you are to your customers,
  the more responsive your business can be to their needs.
  This intimacy can result in creating customers for life.
- **Be on the leading edge and take calculated risks.** A requirement for successful entrepreneurship is finding solutions to people's problems that others don't see. Being a
  market leader gives you a major competitive advantage. All
  of the entrepreneurs profiled in this book are constantly upgrading current products and creating new ones. Going to
  market with a new product is by definition a risk, so it's important that you've done your due diligence and have real
  evidence that the product will sell.
- **Don't let your passion for your product cloud your vision.**
  You may think your idea will change the world, but customers must be willing to buy your product. Be brutally
  honest with yourself and do your homework before you roll
  out a new product.
- **Sometimes being second is best.** Being first of a kind in the
  marketplace positions your company for great rewards.

However, being first also carries more risks since you're learning tough lessons as you go along. Often the most successful products are upgrades of already successful products. When choosing a new product to roll out, consider one that enables you to learn from the successes and failures of others before you.

- **Make your company a reflection of the world.** Our world is a tapestry of ethnic, racial, and cultural diversity, and most companies can benefit from a more diverse staff and customer base. The first step is to make diversity a major business priority, and the second step is to seek guidance and support from others who have had success in this area.

Taking care of customers is not a new concept, nor is valuing the importance of business-customer relationships something fresh and rare. However, building partnerships with your customers to improve your community is a relatively new business strategy. By intentionally building multiple bridges to your customers, you can grow your business and grow local value at the same time.

Building values-driven partnerships with customers is one thing. But how about doing that with the people who provide you with capital? You know that one of your most important roles as the leader of your business is to attract and develop strong financial partnerships. The following chapter points you in an unusual but surprisingly effective direction—building financial partnerships with institutions and people who are committed to growing local value. You'll see how sharing values and a vision with financial partners can be a key strategic advantage and can make a big difference in the community. And it's more fun to boot!

2

Values-based financing

As an entrepreneur, you're well aware that you need capital to make your business vision a reality. For most of us, this means partnering with financial investors. Forging these financial partnerships is one of the most complicated and arduous tasks you'll face as an entrepreneur. This chapter will give you strategic guidance and practical examples that will make this job a bit easier and at the same time help you make a meaningful contribution to your community. You'll see that when values-driven entrepreneurs team with socially conscious investors, they form a powerful combination, and the possibilities for the business and the community are truly limitless.

Choosing the right financial partners has been an underappreciated way for entrepreneurs to contribute to the community. When looking for money, it's natural for you to be more concerned about finding investors than about using your financial partnerships as a way to help the community. But the way you capitalize your business and where you do your banking can make a difference in your community.

Intuitively, you know that it's critical that you find investors who share your values. Partnering with the right investors can be pivotal to your success, while partnering with the wrong investors can seriously damage your business. The capital needed to finance new or expanding small businesses often comes with a hefty price tag, and ideally these dollars should stay in the community and continue to work for it.

Fortunately for entrepreneurs and would-be entrepreneurs, a growing number of individuals, businesses, nonprofits/foundations, and government agencies are investing in well-run local independent businesses. For these community-minded investors, putting money back into the community is intrinsic to their missions. When values-driven investors commit capital to a community-based business, the business wins, the investors win, and the community wins because the flow of money available for other new and expanding values-driven businesses increases.

An excellent example of entrepreneurs successfully partnering with a financial institution committed to the community involves ShoreBank, based in Chicago, Illinois. In 1974 four individuals founded ShoreBank by purchasing a distressed bank with few remaining assets. The founders believed that a commercial bank partnering with complementary development organizations could effectively restore neighborhood economies. Over thirty years later, ShoreBank's operations have demonstrated that a specially designed bank can help reverse the decline of inner-city neighborhoods coping with disinvestment and discrimination.

Since its founding, ShoreBank has invested over $2 billion back into the community, and this reinvestment has been a major factor in its consistent growth. Most loans are made as a part of the bank's mission-related programs in the inner cities of Chicago and Detroit, and a large share of them are made to local entrepreneurs and businesses. ShoreBank has a commitment to make new mission loans each year that total two times its equity capital. In 2005 this amounted to $370 million in new mission loans. What began quite small has grown to hundreds of millions of dollars in loans to local entrepreneurs. This strategy is really quite simple and actually is the original idea behind banks—the more businesses that use community-based banks, the more loans these financial institutions can make to entrepreneurs.

This chapter lists a variety of sources of capital that might fit your entrepreneurial venture. When looking for capital, we recommend keeping the following guidelines in mind:

- Be picky about whom you partner with. Look for financial partners who share your values and are excited about your mission. Don't jump at the first offer to finance your dream. Entrepreneurial tales of businesses getting in bed with a financial institution or private investor that doesn't support their mission, resulting in disastrous consequences, are legion.
- Research all the possible sources of capital available and find financial and legal advisers who can guide you toward appropriate investors and help you structure the deal.
- When making the final decision to work with a financial institution, consider not only your immediate cash needs but, equally important, the quality of the relationship and the potential for obtaining more capital in the future.
- If at all possible, partner with investors who reside in or near your community and have more than a financial stake in your success. This often happens naturally since most investors in a young business do live in the community where the business is located.
- Consider what contributions to the community potential partners will make with the profits from their investment in your company.

Fortunately, if you're up to the challenge of finding financial partners who share your values, the time has never been better to finance a new business. Innovative leaders in the world of finance are engaged in a dynamic and generative conversation focusing specifically on how to get capital into the hands of values-driven entrepreneurs. As a result of this dialogue, creative new structures and investment vehicles are being designed that are opening doors for those entrepreneurs.

Sources of Capital

We have mapped the landscape of sources of capital and identified seven basic categories of potential financial investors: banks and credit unions; venture capital, private equity, and angels; nonprofits and foundations; government agencies; friends and family; business stakeholders; and unconventional financial sources. Each type of investor not only will profit from your success but will make varying degrees of contributions to the community with the profits of your partnership.

Each of the following sources of capital can be more or less appropriate for you based on the type of business you're in and the stage of your business. Start-up businesses generally obtain seed money from family, friends, credit cards, and angel investors. Venture capital usually gets involved in later rounds, after the initial start-up phase and when the product has come to market. Banks generally don't loan money to businesses until they have positive cash flow or an asset that can be used as collateral (for example, real estate).

When considering the various options for raising capital, you need to decide which form of investment best suits your business needs. The two basic types of investments are debt (borrowing money from a bank or other investor) and equity (selling a percentage of ownership in the company to an investor). Both debt and equity have their pros and cons, and many entrepreneurs choose to bring in a combination of debt and equity investments.

Banks and Credit Unions

Banks are generally not inclined to finance business start-ups. Even mature businesses searching for capital to expand have had the experience of knocking on bankers' doors and hearing a politely phrased response that essentially says, "We only lend money to companies that don't need money." This proves to be true even for banks that advertise their love for small businesses.

On the bright side, some banks loan money to businesses that really need it, and an increasing number of credit unions are moving into commercial lending. These forward-thinking banks and credit unions approve loans based on solid business plans and on their belief in a product and the entrepreneur. Smart lenders base each decision on relationships and a deep understanding of the business rather than a blind adherence to one formula or another. And the degree to which a bank or credit union contributes to the community varies widely—both in the loans and in the charitable contributions it makes. Your job as an entrepreneur is to find those financial institutions that are willing to do business with you and come closest to matching your values.

A common approach to raising capital is to work with a bank to secure a loan through government agencies such as the Small Business Administration (SBA), which guarantees small business loans up to $2 million. Other government agencies are structured to loan larger amounts to certain qualified businesses. You also may want to hire a broker to assist you in connecting your business with the right combination of financial investors.

Commercial Banks

Commercial banking has gone through massive convolutions over the past ten years. Not long ago, working in banking was considered one of the most stable jobs. Today, banks are being merged and bought out at breakneck speed, and bank employees have little job security. This employment instability means that entrepreneurs often have difficulty establishing strong and lasting relationships with commercial bank lenders. Commercial banks come in three basic sizes, and each size offers different types of service for an entrepreneur.

- *Multinational banks.* For some reason, multinational banks always seem to be increasing their already massive size, even though their customers (and staff members) are still reeling from the chaos created by the previous merger or acquisition. Consequently, these banks generally have a revolving staff and it's difficult to develop personal relationships with them. Furthermore, it's also true that when two major banks merge, their combined charitable contributions usually decrease. All this being said, multinational banks do make loans to small companies, and depending on the particular bank, region, and loan officer, this may be a short-term option for you. However, for numerous reasons we recommend this be your last choice when choosing a banker.
- *Large, regional banks.* Regional banks may be a good choice. Unfortunately, they are a dying breed and the ones that remain are constantly under threat of acquisition by larger banks. An excellent example of an entrepreneur-friendly regional bank is Silicon Valley Bank. It offers flexible options for early-stage companies (particularly technology companies) and makes loans that may be tied to equity ownership. If you're considering doing business with a regional bank, speak with entrepreneurs who do business with it and ask about it at local nonprofits and community groups. These references are essential when beginning a

banking relationship. Also, it's always a good practice to meet with the lender within the bank who would be your account officer and discuss how lending decisions are made and by whom.

- *Small, local banks.* Local banks are often excellent corporate citizens because they view themselves as important parts of their communities, which is the very nature of being a local bank. They are generally the best choice if you want to borrow from a commercial bank. It's refreshing to walk into your bank and see the president working near the lobby. More important, it's sweet when you have a partner who views it as his or her job to help you succeed and who gains pleasure from your growth and success. On the downside, small, local banks tend to be conservative and may be unwilling to take risks on new, innovative ventures. This too is changing as they are becoming more entrepreneurial and thus more entrepreneur-friendly in order to remain competitive. The bottom line is that an entrepreneur's relationship with a small bank can be wonderful.

Savings Banks and Cooperative Banks

Savings banks and cooperative banks are some of the first places you might visit when looking for a loan. They are owned by their customers, and their boards are made up of local people. If they were to be sold, no one person or management team would benefit, and consequently they generally remain independent and aren't targets for acquisition. Their charters state that their purpose is to support the local community. They tend to reflect the personality and values of the president and/or board and usually consider the value of a company to the community when making loans. Your job is to find a savings bank in your community that likes your product and believes in you.

Credit Unions

In some communities, credit unions have become legitimate sources of capital for businesses. A legendary example is Vancity Savings Credit Union in Vancouver, British Columbia, which has been a longtime values-driven business leader. Vancity has a strong commitment to its community and champions the importance of small businesses. Consider credit unions as potential financial partners when you're looking for capital.

Venture Capital, Private Equity, and Angels

Firms and individuals who specialize in capitalizing start-ups and expansions of young businesses represent a relatively new phenomenon and have played a pivotal role in the growth of entrepreneurial ventures in the United States. These firms and individuals invest in companies with different combinations of debt and equity, different expectations for a return, and a broad diversity in values.

Traditional Venture Capital Firms

Venture capital firms occasionally invest in early-stage companies, but generally they get involved in the second or third round of financing after the business case has been proven. Although venture capital firms do not necessarily require a company to be cash positive, they do expect it to have customers and commitments for more business before they will invest. More than 70 percent of venture capital firms fund technology and biotech, so other industries have less of a chance to receive funding from them.

Most venture capital firms require a major (if not controlling) interest in the business. Because their business model assumes a percentage of investment failures, they require fast growth, a very high rate of return, and a relatively quick exit strategy, which places great stress on the business. And on top of these negatives, they don't pay great attention to values. However, a growing number of venture capital firms have adopted a commitment to job creation and community values and are more entrepreneur-friendly.

Community Development Venture Capital Funds (CDVC)

Community development venture capital funds are a growing form of investment utilizing both debt and equity options. They combine a commitment to community development with the tools of traditional venture capital and offer a possible solution to the thousands of promising new companies that fall through the investment screen of traditional venture capital firms. Developmental venture capital funds deploy venture capital on a smaller scale, making it possible to foster a whole tier of investments in smaller companies that do not meet the standard criteria. In 2000 the average CDVC fund investment was $331,000 per company. Although these funds tend to operate in a wider range of industries, they rigorously practice conventional venture financing disciplines in order to accomplish their purposes.

The Community Development Venture Capital Alliance (CDVCA) is a national association of fifty-five member venture capital funds, community development corporations, and others who promote the use of venture capital tools to create jobs, entrepreneurial capacity, and wealth to advance the livelihood of distressed communities. CDVCA funds are mission-driven organizations established explicitly to benefit distressed communities and regions. According to CDVCA, at least ninety-five community development venture funds exist or are being formed throughout the world, with more than $500 million under management domestically. This form of investment may be just the ticket for financing part or all of your new venture or expansion.

Private Equity Funds

Private equity funds are pools of money dedicated to investment in privately held companies. These funds come in many varieties. For example, buyout firms acquire companies, "dress them up" (usually by dramatically cutting costs), and offer them for sale either to another private buyer or via an initial public offering. Longer-term private equity funds seek to own a minority interest in private companies. In today's innovative investment world, an increasing number of firms are interested in long-term investments and consider the interests of all stakeholders. Main Street Resources of Westport, Connecticut, is a terrific example of a values-driven private equity firm that takes the long view and has as its mission to support the growth and increase the value of small and midsized companies.

Angel Investors

Angel investors are the largest source of seed and start-up capital. According to a study done by the Kauffman Foundation, approximately 225,000 angels are investing roughly $20 billion per year and funding around 50,000 entrepreneurial ventures, with an average of four to five investors joining forces per deal.[4]

Values-driven angel investors have played a pivotal role in the growth and development of many socially responsible companies. The leading example of a network of socially conscious angel investors is Investors' Circle (IC). IC was founded in 1992 by a group of SVN members who wanted to share information about values-driven investment opportunities and possibly pool their resources to make deals work. It is filling an important need, and since its inception, IC has invested an estimated $100 million in over 160 companies. Under the leadership of Woody Tasch, this dynamic network is cultivating an investment culture of patient capital and experimenting with nontraditional ways to invest in values-driven businesses.

Other local angel investor networks in North America, both formal and informal, are looking to invest in values-driven companies. We highly recommend making values-driven angels one of your priorities when searching for start-up capital.

Nonprofits and Foundations

Nonprofits and foundations have only recently entered the world of venture financing and participate in a small percentage of new entrepreneurial deals. Nonetheless, opportunities for developing financial partnerships are growing, and values-driven entrepreneurs should look for nonprofits and foundations that might be a good match.

Community Development Corporations

Community development corporations (CDCs) are nonprofit organizations formed to support community development in low-income communities. They are known more for financing low-income housing; however, recently more CDCs are seeing the importance of supporting the growth of a strong local business community. CDCs are set up to receive funding from federal, state, and local governments, and several now offer grants and loans to businesses operating in underserved communities.

Quasi-Governmental Organizations

As political leaders and government organizations recognize the importance of strong local businesses, quasi-governmental agencies are being developed that help finance local business development. The Community Development Finance Corporation is an example of a quasi-governmental organization that helps finance ventures in low-income areas.

Foundations

Foundations are slowly entering the world of investing in values-driven businesses. Their investments, known as program-related investments (PRIs), are usually in the form of debt rather than equity. Foundations invest in companies that they think will make a substantial and direct impact on the communities they are committed to improving. We are aware of some notable examples of foundations making high-risk investments that bankers or investors could never make. In fact, for a foundation to make a PRI, the venture must include a high degree of risk. As values-driven commerce grows, an increasing number of innovative foundations will make PRIs, though today they provide but a tiny portion of capital invested in companies.

Social Finance Organizations

An emerging source of capital for entrepreneurs consists of nonprofit organizations that some are calling social finance organizations. These nonprofits pool individual and institutional investor funds and make equity investments or loans, and they will likely play an increasingly important role as a source of social capital. As mission-driven entities, social finance organizations, like RSF, strive to provide help in areas underserved by conventional financial institutions, such as early-stage capital for social enterprises, technical expertise, and capital structure assistance.

Microlending Institutions

"Microlending" is a term that originally described tiny loans to artisans and craftspeople in undeveloped nations. Recently, some institutions in the United States have been set up to offer small loans to low-income sole proprietors and help small shop owners get their start.

City, County, State, and Federal Government Agencies

In recent years, local municipalities and state governments have used grants, loans, and tax incentives (sometimes using federal funds) to attract businesses and keep them in their communities. Historically, most of these funds have been given to large corporations. Fortunately, community leaders are beginning to recognize that providing grants and loans to locally owned, independent small businesses may be a more effective strategy for long-term economic development.

When municipalities invest in local companies, they may do it for job creation, environmental benefits, inner-city revitalization, Main Street and retail support, or general economic development. We suggest scouring the landscape to identify what kind of financing is available for your particular type of business in your local community.

In addition, several federal government programs support small business development. The best known is the SBA, which was mentioned earlier in this chapter, but others exist and are worth looking into, such as the United States Department of Agriculture (USDA).

Friends and Family

Family and friends are one of the top sources of early-stage funding for entrepreneurial ventures. And this pool of potential investors isn't limited to simply your immediate family and close friends but also includes their extended families and friends too. When family and friends invest in your business, they share in its financial success and the community benefits. And it keeps the money moving throughout the community. People who make profitable investments in entrepreneurial endeavors often make repeat investments and encourage others to do the same.

But many potential entrepreneurs don't have the personal connections necessary to bankroll a start-up venture. This is particularly true for people of color and those starting a business in an inner-city area. Fortunately, groups such as the Social Impact Leadership Coalition (a group that SVN organized) and the Initiative for a Competitive Inner City (ICIC) have as one of their objectives "to democratize entrepreneurship" by supporting and promoting programs that assist entrepreneurs of color in starting and growing businesses.

Business Stakeholders

When an entrepreneur forms financial partnerships with local business stakeholders, the profits from their investments stay in the community, and local people are rewarded for their faith and the risk they take. People who have a stake in the continued existence of a business feel good about using their money to support it and personally benefit from the myriad of contributions the company makes to the community.

Vendors

In many business sectors (retail, for example), vendors traditionally are important financial partners to entrepreneurs, and both parties and the community can benefit from the relationship. If a company is given even thirty days to pay after a product is delivered, that in effect is a thirty-day loan from the vendor. In some cases, the vendor will agree to stretch the terms to ninety days, and it's not uncommon for a retailer to have a continuous and growing outstanding balance with a vendor. This account payable becomes a no-cost or low-cost loan to the business, and the vendor becomes a significant financial partner.

Another popular method of obtaining financing is to lease equipment (or establish a payment plan) directly from the vendor, distributor, or manufacturer.

As vendors have begun to look for creative ways to increase sales and nurture customer relationships, some of them have developed programs that actually help finance the business of potentially high-volume customers.

Contractors and Business Customers

If an entrepreneur determines that the success of his or her business is dependent on a specific vendor, he or she may consider investing in this important partner. Judy Wicks, founder of the White Dog Cafe (see chapter 4), is an entrepreneur who made it her business to make a financial investment in her vendors. She did this through personal loans and grants from a foundation she set up. These investments have helped ensure the health and long-term success of her own company.

Fellow Business Owners

Entrepreneurs in the same industry get to know each other while working together on various projects. They all understand the industry and what it takes to succeed. When you develop a relationship with a successful fellow entrepreneur, making an investment may be a natural step to take.

Customers

It makes perfect sense that your satisfied customers would want to invest in a product they love and a company they trust. When you are working on creative strategies for raising capital, customers are excellent prospects to enlist as financial partners.

If you're in a start-up mode, you may not have any customers yet. But if you're becoming an entrepreneur after having worked for another business in the same or related industry, your past customers may be potential investors. If you're looking to expand your business, then going to your customers may be a great option. For example, the Longfellow Clubs has financed twenty years of expansion projects primarily through financial partnerships with customers. When community residents share in the financial rewards of your business, the community clearly benefits. Furthermore, this group of customers is more deeply and financially committed to your success.

Staff

One of the more interesting developments in today's investment world is that staff members of a small business may have greater financial resources than the entrepreneur. Your staff members have much at stake in the survival and growth of your business, and if they feel a sense of ownership they will often offer help when your business needs capital. These investments can be in the form of promissory notes or actual ownership. Ownership options include the increasingly popular employee stock ownership plans. When you involve your employees in the financing of your business, they will have more at stake and have another tangible way to share in the financial success of your company.

Unconventional Financing

Credit card companies, equipment leasing companies, and other unconventional financing sources such as factoring companies (companies that specialize in lending money based on accounts receivable) are not known for making contributions to the community. In addition, their interest rates are normally extremely high and their terms may be onerous. It's interesting to note that a recent survey done by the Initiative for a Competitive Inner City discovered that by far the most popular way to finance start-ups in inner-city communities is through credit cards.[5] Anecdotally, we've found that to be true for entrepreneurs everywhere. As we know, when entrepreneurs need cash, they will go to extraordinary lengths to track down capital to start or expand their businesses.

The profusion of capital sources accessible to values-driven entrepreneurs is opening new doors for you and your business and bodes well for your future growth. The abundance of available sources of capital gives you many choices and is another reason for carefully examining the mission and practices of all the people or institutions you choose to bring in as financial partners. City Fresh Foods, Small Potatoes Urban Delivery, and ANSCO Real Estate Investments are three companies that provide excellent examples of how financial partnerships can work for a business, reward the financial partners, and grow local value.

Partnering with Investors:
City Fresh Foods, Roxbury, Massachusetts

Glynn and Sheldon Lloyd are young African-American brothers who serve as role models for entrepreneurs who want to make a difference in inner-city communities. Their story is a classic case study of the financing challenges entrepreneurs face, the creative means they employ to meet these challenges, and the ways the solutions can benefit the community. Futhermore, the City Fresh model stands as an example of how a company's social mission can be pivotal in developing financial partnerships that enable it to secure financing.

Glynn Lloyd founded City Fresh Foods in 1994 as a catering service for local government agencies and civic groups. This work led him to seeing an even larger need in his community—nutritious meals served in programs and schools for young people and seniors that met the tastes of Boston's various ethnic communities. In early 1995 City Fresh obtained its first contract with Central Boston Elder Services to provide 100 Latin meals a day. Twelve years later, City Fresh is serving over 4,000 hot meals, 1,200 breakfasts, and 400 snacks a day and has revenues of $4 million. In 2006 it was included on *Inc.* magazine's Inner City 100 list of fastest-growing urban companies.[6]

Glynn's vision has become reality—an inner-city business having its production facility and offices located in the community, employing a diverse population from the community, and meeting important nutrition needs of seniors and youth. It's the only food service company in the nation that offers senior nutrition programs a variety of traditional and ethnic Latin, Caribbean, and Russian menus to choose from. City Fresh also provides and delivers to schools, day-care centers, and after-school programs cost-effective breakfast, snack, and lunch menus that meet U.S. Department of Agriculture Student Guidelines. City Fresh's mission statement is

> We prepare traditional and ethnic, home-style meals for senior nutrition programs, schools, and community organizations.
>
> Behind our delicious food is a successful business model that incorporates community and economic development. We believe that business is a powerful vehicle for empowering our youth, developing the community, and nurturing the environment.

Finding capital to start and grow a business can be a monumental challenge. When you're an African-American entrepreneur starting a business in the inner city and you have no real financial assets yourself, the job of finding capital becomes Herculean. Tracking the trail of capital that fed the growth of City Fresh offers important lessons in entrepreneurial resourcefulness. It also reveals the dialectical nature of our economic system—a wide variety of capital sourcing alternatives is available to entrepreneurs, but serious structural barriers remain that prevent entrepreneurs from starting and growing a business, particularly one in the inner city.

Glynn capitalized his business by applying for and receiving a job creation grant for $20,000 from the Business Development Office of the City of Boston. He then leveraged that grant to obtain a loan from Nuestra Comunidad Development Corporation for $10,000, bringing his start-up capital to $30,000.

These funds allowed Glynn to open his first kitchen in a high crime area and begin to cook meals to fulfill his first contract. It was not an easy environment in which to start a business. When deliveries came, two people had to meet the delivery truck—one to bring in the food and the other one to stand guard to make sure no one walked off with the food they had just unloaded.

City Fresh's first contract was with an agency of the City of Boston, and to this day the majority of its contracts are with government organizations. This aspect of Glynn's business plan generated major cash flow challenges for City Fresh because a business is lucky if a government agency pays within forty-five days. Usually it's much later. On the flip side, City Fresh employees were paid weekly, and in the early days all deliveries were cash on delivery. Cash came in slowly and cash went out quickly—the definition of a cash flow problem.

To alleviate the problem, Glynn would show up at the city offices and charm and beg staff to mail the checks within fifteen days. However, as the company grew, a line of credit to pay bills became necessary to keep accounts payable current while waiting for accounts receivable checks from the government to arrive. Not surprisingly, no bank Glynn talked to would even consider a loan of this nature because the business was too young and had little collateral. Having no wealthy family or friends to lean on, he was forced to turn to a factoring company for a loan that used accounts receivable as collateral and charged very high interest rates and fees.

Over time Glynn became a master in the art of entrepreneurial juggling, and he somehow managed to get through the first year and survive the high cost of money. By the end of 1995 he had developed a track record of sound management and consistent growth, which enabled City Fresh to obtain a $150,000 line of credit from the Urban Initiative Fund (UIF), a Community Development Finance Corporation. UIF is a quasi-governmental agency that was formed to support inner-city economic development after the Rodney King riots. This line of credit put City Fresh on a more solid footing and provided the financial foundation for the company's next growth spurt.

By 1998 Glynn's brother Sheldon had come on board as chief financial officer, and the company was doing better but still barely breaking even. The brothers were working long hours and making below minimum wage (a familiar story for entrepreneurs). As is the case with most business plans, the City Fresh plan required a certain volume to ensure financial stability—the company had to grow. This growth in sales in turn demanded that the brothers expand their plant. To do this they needed more capital. And even with a positive track record, no commercial bank would help them.

This was frustrating, but not to be deterred, the Lloyd brothers demonstrated their resilient spirit and muscular will by cobbling together a creative combination of investors. They found a new inner-city location that was previously unused and signed a lease with the City of Boston and simultaneously obtained a storefront loan from the city for $25,000 to help renovate the building. Still needing cash to complete the expansion, Glynn and Sheldon connected with two community-oriented institutions: Boston Community Capital (BCC), a community development venture capital firm, and the Institute for Civil Society (ICS), a nonprofit foundation. These two organizations were excited about this young venture and together made an equity investment of $190,000, which enabled City Fresh to complete the remodeling and purchase new equipment.

With this expansion complete, City Fresh was able to continue its growth and become profitable. The brothers were now looking for more traditional financing at lower interest rates. Again they employed some imaginative strategies. Their new building had been taken over by the city, and they were able to negotiate an excellent purchase price. Working with a supportive bank officer at a regional bank, they leveraged their newly purchased real estate and obtained a mortgage for $260,000 at an interest rate of 8 percent. They used this money to buy back the preferred stock of BCC and ICS, which decreased their annual debt service and dramatically improved cash flow.

Now that they had reduced their monthly debt service, they encountered yet another cash flow problem. The higher their sales volume, the higher the line of credit they required. By 2000 City Fresh was growing 30 percent a year and needed an expanded credit line.

The brothers went back to their bank and, to their surprise, discovered that their friendly regional bank had been purchased by an international bank and that their new loan officer didn't share the values of the previous one. According to the bank's new formula, City Fresh no longer qualified for the line of credit. The bank had loaned City Fresh capital, which was used to buy back the preferred stock. Because City Fresh was paying very high dividends (at an interest rate of 15 percent) before the refinancing, this buyback greatly strengthened the company by improving cash flow significantly. But from the bank's point of view, City Fresh now had a mortgage on the building, so its debt was higher and it no longer met the bank's required debt-to-equity ratio. Only after much complaining and cajoling did the Lloyd brothers persuade this supposedly "small business–friendly" bank to give them the $195,000 line of credit they needed.

Glynn and Sheldon are now looking around for a small, community-oriented, local bank that understands their business, appreciates their mission, and is genuinely interested in being a worthy business partner.

All of their trials and tribulations have brought out the best in both brothers. Sheldon has become a highly skilled CFO and is playing a pivotal role in the company's growth. Besides continuing as CEO, Glynn is now active in supporting other business leaders committed to inner-city economic development and is in the process of building a new business focusing on healthy activities for children.

Bootstrapping Is Tough Business

When asked what mistakes he made and what he learned from the adventures of financing City Fresh Foods, Glynn responds with one word: "undercapitalized." Like many entrepreneurs, the Lloyd brothers bootstrapped their business with very little cash.

As mentioned earlier, Glynn started the business by borrowing $30,000, and he retained 100 percent ownership. After Sheldon joined him, they brought in equity partners and were able to maintain the majority of stock in their company. Most entrepreneurs are understandably reticent to give up control of their business. After all, the energy unleashed from entrepreneurial freedom is what enables entrepreneurs to do what it takes to make the business work. City Fresh has become a locally owned community institution, and Glynn and Sheldon feel good about this. But starting the business without financial backing from partners took its emotional and physical toll—it was an all-consuming process filled with crises.

Fortunately, "going it alone" at the beginning ultimately worked for Glynn and Sheldon, but more often than not, undercapitalization is the demise of many young businesses. If they were to do it over again, the Lloyd brothers would search out values-driven investors and institutions that understood their mission and were willing to become financial partners. It's much easier to develop financial partnerships and raise capital before you begin a business than it is when you're desperate and in the middle of a cash flow crisis.

Glynn is starting up a new business in Boston that offers inner city youth a fun, healthy, and educational place to relax, play, and have birthday parties. This time around, he has raised the capital in advance of opening the business. This working capital will enable his company to handle the inevitable cash flow shortages, unpredictable crises, and management misjudgments. It's important that your business plan make conservative projections and attempt to anticipate possible problems. Still, even the best business plans can't predict all the problems that will occur. New ventures are cash hogs, and working capital needs to be available to get a company through its volatile early stages. When you start a new business, the last bit of capital needed can be the most difficult to rope in. But the cushion it provides serves as a lifeline during those pressure-filled early years.

Balancing the Needs of Entrepreneurs with the Needs of Financial Partners

Glynn and Sheldon have successfully partnered with investors who shared their commitment to supporting the cultural and economic life of the inner city. However, even in the best financial partnerships where everyone shares the same values, financial negotiations can be tricky. The City Fresh story illustrates some of the complexities you might face when partnering with investors.

In the early years, City Fresh Foods had major challenges obtaining sufficient financing. The company was too young, was not profitable, was located in an inner-city community, and had no collateral. Glynn's networking skills brought him in contact with two institutions that shared his mission to build a livable, safe, and strong inner city of Boston: BCC and ICS.

BCC and ICS were captivated by the Lloyd brothers and their mission, and they decided to cooperatively invest in City Fresh Foods and finance its next phase of growth. They also offered to bring in advisers to give City Fresh guidance on how to deal with the many hurdles placed before them. Glynn and

Sheldon were excited to find financial partners who shared their values and had a commitment to grow local value in the inner city of Boston. It meant that the return on investment City Fresh gave its financial partners would be used to support other values-driven entrepreneurs and community ventures rather than big banks or large institutional investors.

The financial structure of a young business can become quite complicated because the needs of the entrepreneur must be balanced with the needs of the financial partners. Even when partners share common values, the specifics of a deal can raise a number of questions, such as

- What is the risk for the investors?
- Who has control of the company?
- Will certain covenants need to be set?
- What is an appropriate interest rate and/or ownership percentage for the investors?
- What is the balance of debt versus equity?
- What is the exit strategy for the financial partners?

Businesspeople experienced in financing small businesses have developed guidelines that effectively and equitably address the above questions. The deal between City Fresh and BCC/ICS offers an excellent example of a deal that may not meet all the needs of both parties but can serve as a model for resolving this entrepreneur-investor tension.

In return for investing $190,000, BCC received 18 percent and ICS 9 percent of the company's common stock, as well as preferred stock valued at $190,000 that paid an average interest rate of 15 percent. On top of this, the preferred stockholders could select two board members, the Lloyd brothers could select two, and the fifth member would be appointed by joint agreement of the Lloyd brothers and the participating investors. One important aspect of the deal was that the capital was in the form of preferred stock, and this (unlike debt) strengthened the balance sheet considerably.

In the end, did this deal result in the classic win-win result? Both parties have great respect for each other and feel good about the original deal. BCC and ICS feel they took a major risk on a young start-up and are thrilled to see City Fresh grow and thrive. Their relatively high interest rates are necessary to ensure their investors receive a fair return on their investment. The returns need to be high enough to cover the losses from other investments they make in start-up ventures that don't succeed.

Eight years later, Glynn and Sheldon are appreciative to have made a deal that took much pressure off them and enabled their company to survive and grow. After being paid very high interest rates and having 100 percent of their investment paid back, BCC and ICS remain City Fresh stockholders and board members. The Lloyds sometimes wonder if the price was too high and where the "social mission" part of this investment was. The answer to this question is important. When social mission investors make investments, they do so within general guidelines and rules of the financial world: investors need to receive a fair return, they need to be able to exit within a fairly short time frame, and they need to have a reward commensurate with the risk they take. The deal may not have been a perfect one, but both brothers acknowledge that the fact that BCC and ICS even made the investment in their company (after banks had turned them down) demonstrated great faith in City Fresh and support for the community. In addition, the expert guidance and business support they received proved to be invaluable. When all is said and done, the investment was beneficial to both parties and the community continues to reap daily rewards through this successful financial partnership.

Best Practices in Partnering with Investors

Like Glynn and Sheldon Lloyd, David Van Seters is an entrepreneur who knows how to raise money. In fact, David's been packaging and selling opportunities for investing in his business for as long as he's been in business.

Partnering with Socially Conscious Investors: Small Potatoes Urban Delivery, Vancouver, British Columbia

David Van Seters is an innovative entrepreneur who not only built a company that contributes to the community but makes a further impact by partnering with socially conscious investors. While working for years as an environmental management consultant, David sensed a vision for a new business bubbling up within him. His vision combined four business trends: leveraging the Internet, catering to customers' needs, selling locally grown organic food, and helping preserve the environment. In 1998 he founded Small Potatoes Urban Delivery (SPUD) in Vancouver, British Columbia, with the following mission:

> To be the most socially responsible, environmentally sound, and financially profitable Internet home delivery company in North America while simplifying and enriching the lives of our customers, staff, suppliers, and community partners.

After eight years of doing business, SPUD has been profitable for the last four years and has grown to become a $10 million business, making 3,500 deliveries a week in four locations: Vancouver, Victoria, Calgary, and Seattle. With seventy-five employees, SPUD is the largest organic and the largest stand-alone grocery delivery firm in Canada. Its five-year business plan calls for doing $50 million in sales and growing by two locations every year.

When David began SPUD, he was well versed in the intricacies of local organic food systems, but a novice when it came to raising money. Now he is a leading example of an entrepreneur who has been able to raise significant capital from socially conscious investors and still maintain control of his company.

SPUD's substantial growth required that David spend much of his time raising funds because his primary source of capital has been short-term promissory notes, which often need to be repaid in a year or two. Each year he has needed to raise more capital than the last, from $200,000 in 2000 to over $1 million in 2006. He has done this by selling the mission of SPUD to financial investors who share his values. In fact, David feels that although he provides a good return on investment, the primary motivating factor of his capital partners is their desire to promote local and organic food systems.

He got SPUD jump-started with $150,000 of his own money. A year later he brought in Joel Solomon of Renewal Partners, who put up $120,000—$70,000 in stock and $50,000 in debt. Renewal Partners is a group of professional angel investors who endeavor to help build a network of entrepreneurial businesses that have a strong social purpose and make a contribution toward a long-term, conservation-centered economy in British Columbia. Not only did bringing in this respected firm as a lead investor provide SPUD with capital and helpful guidance, but equally important, it introduced SPUD to a network of other investors.

Subsequent investors have been individuals David met through his networking, including Investors' Circle and Social Venture Institute (a joint SVN and Renewal Partners program). David raised $400,000 from a local bank, which he has since repaid. SPUD also has two lines of credit with socially responsible local credit unions in Vancouver—Vancity and Coast Capital.

David looks for financial partners who support the SPUD vision, and he devised an investment strategy that would make it relatively easy to invest in SPUD and just as simple to exit. He did this by offering convertible debentures (a type of debt) that could be converted to stock after one year or rolled over into a new two-year note. The interest rates varied between 6 percent and 12 percent based on the size of the investment—the larger the investment, the higher the interest.

It is generally easier to raise short-term debt (debt due in five years or less) because the exit strategy is clear. But an obvious problem is that investors can choose to opt out after the term of the debenture and need to be paid back then. Usually a young company's cash flow isn't strong enough to cover substantial repayment of debt, and this generally means raising more capital every year to pay investors back or risk being in default. In the case of SPUD, every year an average of 50 percent of the investors have opted to get their money back and SPUD has repaid over $1 million in principal to debenture holders.

At the beginning of each year, David and his management team calculate the debt service the company can realistically handle and the repayment of principal required and then set the amount of capital they will raise for expansion. As of May 2006, Renewal Partners (the second largest stockholder) owned 16 percent of the stock, several individual investors converted their debentures to a cumulative total of 33 percent of the stock, and David retained 51 percent of the stock in the business. David is now contemplating how much equity he is willing to sell. Like so many values-driven entrepreneurs, he is concerned more about control than about money. Since he feels aligned with his investors and has developed such deep trust in them, he is leaning toward giving up another 10 percent of the business in order to meet his growth objectives.

David's long-term financing strategy for SPUD is to make the company so attractive that he can sell a minority portion of the business to a friendly investor at a high price and buy out all the convertible debentures. He's also looking into various forms of employee ownership that would reward current employees and tie managers of new locations more closely to the business. Currently all staff members participate in a profit-sharing plan and have the opportunity to purchase discounted shares of the company.

When asked about his choice to become an entrepreneur and spend so much time raising capital, David responded, "SPUD has proven that a strong social and environmental ethic is good for business, and while SPUD has been a very challenging business, I cannot think of any other work I would rather do. We have a great team of talented and dedicated people who truly believe that we can change the world, one grocery order at a time. What more could one ask for?"

Andy Schcolnik feels the same way, only his business works to change the world one rehabbed inner-city building at a time. The Lloyd brothers and David Van Seters are in the food business, which has its own particular financing complications. When you're in the construction business, financing is a bit more straightforward. You're generally looking for bank financing since the real estate provides the necessary collateral. Andy Schcolnik grew local value by partnering with one of North America's most community-minded banks, ShoreBank. The result has been a strong business and an improved community.

Partnering with a Local Bank Committed to the Community: ANSCO Real Estate, Chicago, Illinois

Andy Schcolnik is an Argentine immigrant who began his business, ANSCO Real Estate Investments, in Chicago in 1991. He borrowed $17,000 from his parents and purchased a dilapidated three-unit residential building that had been foreclosed on in an impoverished community. He got it at the rock-bottom price of $17,000 because no one else showed up at the auction.

With his own labor he rehabbed the building and rented the units as government-subsidized housing.

Since the rental income provided him with a positive cash flow, he wanted to expand his business, but every bank turned him down because he had no credit. Fortunately, because he was creating affordable housing in a predominantly African-American community, a local African-American owned bank loaned him enough money to pay off his debt and have $20,000 left to purchase more properties.

By 1995 he had branched out into condo conversions, working with a variety of design options and upgrading the quality of his construction. His company is now doing about $6 million a year in business and has a construction team of around 50 employees. ANSCO Construction, LLC, has built over 400 units of good quality, affordable housing for lower-middle-class people (mostly African Americans) who normally wouldn't have been able to become homeowners.

The company's success has much to do with Andy's partnership with a community-based bank. In 2000, after ANSCO had established a strong track record, Andy borrowed $250,000 from ShoreBank. This was the beginning of a long and mutually beneficial relationship. ShoreBank was founded with the mission of "investing in people and their communities to create economic equity" and has long been a major player in economic development on the south side of Chicago.

Andy has found ShoreBank to be a friendly and supportive partner and he has received $12 million in loans. In his words, the bank has "intuitive and gutsy lenders that approved loans based not only on the deal but on the individual." His bank officer, Jim Bringley, who manages the real estate division, is just one example. He, like ShoreBank itself, believes in revitalizing low-income neighborhoods and has made it an important priority.

ShoreBank also partnered with Andy on his vision to revitalize the Grand Ballroom, a major landmark in the Woodlawn neighborhood of Chicago. Andy has earned much acclaim for his adaptive reuse of this historic building, which had sat vacant and deteriorating for nearly a decade.

This restoration was the biggest challenge his company had faced, and Andy recalls the times he went back to Jim and admitted that he was up to two times over the original budget. Jim was understanding and offered support and suggested possible alternatives. Like so many restorations, this project grew to be much larger than anticipated. But the risk and hard work paid off because the beautiful renovated Grand Ballroom has become a magnet for economic and cultural activity in this area of Chicago. The newly restored, mixed-use Grand Ballroom is now a premier party space and home to much-needed neighborhood retail shops, including the Inspiration Cafe, which provides training for homeless and disadvantaged residents that helps them enter the workplace.

Lessons Learned: Partnering with Investors

Obtaining the capital your business needs can be a complicated process. The rules of finance are changing rapidly, and nearly every week a new investment vehicle is in the works. We are all on a continuous learning curve, and the stories in this chapter offer you some simple yet valuable lessons for financing or refinancing your business:

- **Seize the time.** Now more than ever, a profusion of potential sources of capital is available. A passionate and skilled entrepreneur with a good idea can put together the financial structures that meet the needs of both the company and the investors. Make it your intention to partner with investors who share your values and believe in your business.

- **Bank with a friend.** Do your banking with financial institutions that treat you right, value you as a customer, and give back to the community. By supporting a bank involved in the community, you are growing local value. Values-driven bankers exist and it's your job to find one.

- **Consider developing a strategic alliance.** A partnership with another business or experienced entrepreneur could let you stay in control of your business while providing the resources your venture needs. This partnership could take many forms, but it's important that your new partner be committed to your company mission and offer your company the financial, intellectual, and spiritual strength it needs to thrive.

- **"Show me the money" first.** It's highly preferable to raise the working capital you need before you go into business. Not having a financial cushion can be lethal because it's not easy raising money to make payroll after you're in business. Unfortunately, unexpected problems come up, and undercapitalization is the single biggest reason for business failures.

You have seen how attracting financial partners who are committed to building bridges with the community can play a pivotal role in the success and growth of your business. The next chapter showcases extraordinary examples of how entrepreneurs have partnered with their staff to enhance the community and, in the process, have strengthened their businesses as well.

3

Partnering with your employees

Staff members are the heart and soul of a company. They create the product and deliver it to the customer, and their skills and attitude make or break a business. In fact, when you get right down to it, the very essence of your company culture and the values you hold dear are expressed through your employees.

It's no secret that building strong and vibrant relationships with your employees is essential for business success! The futures of your business and your staff are bound together, and it only makes sense to move your business-staff relationship to the level of partnership. The strongest partnerships are those in which both parties have much to lose and much to gain. The larger the stakes, the greater the potential for a robust partnership—and your employees have a great deal at stake in the success of your business. Having a satisfying and well-paying job is essential to living a good life. Full-time employees structure their lives around their jobs and spend a majority of their waking hours (and usually their most productive time) working for the business and giving their creative energy. For longtime employees, building the company can become their career or even their life's work. Our careers say much about how we think about ourselves and greatly influence our self-esteem.

It's a simple equation. Your company depends on the staff to carry out its mission, while the employees depend on the business for their livelihood. When both parties view this relationship as a partnership, the benefits to both are significant. The Longfellow Clubs has established a business-staff covenant that makes explicit the depth of the partnership and goes beyond a legal contract: "Longfellow will do everything it can to support staff members in reaching their full potential as whole human beings. Staff members will do all they can do to support Longfellow in achieving its mission."

By placing support for your staff members squarely in the center of the company's core values, you have the best chance of building an inspired and fully engaged team. Staff members feel better about themselves and become more dedicated to the company's mission. Our experience has been that it's a one-to-one correlation—the happier the staff, the more successful the business.

Developing a strong partnership with staff members naturally leads to community contributions. It's safe to say that if you want your company to make a difference in the community, your staff will be your most direct and reliable link. A business filled with satisfied employees committed to serving customers and meeting community needs becomes a valued resource for the community.

Another added benefit of having a staff involved in building a healthy community is the synergy it creates. There's no better way to build staff loyalty than to engage staff members in community work. The pride they develop in their business becomes palpable, and company loyalty flows organically into the hearts of your associates.

You can increase profits and strengthen your community by partnering with employees in the following ways:

- *Provide quality jobs.* Rooting your business in the community and creating well-paying and satisfying jobs is one of the most important ways you can serve your community. We have seen large companies shedding jobs and either moving out of town or being acquired by even bigger corporations. Though the government and the media tend to focus on the comings and goings of multinational corporations, the small and midsized companies run by entrepreneurs are the real engines of job growth in the United States. Growing your business locally and increasing your payroll makes a big difference in your community and substantially grows local value.
- *Set up shop in underserved communities.* Building a business in an underserved community such as an inner city or a poor rural area can help turn that community around. Not only do these communities have large pools of employable residents who need good jobs, but companies can work with government agencies to train and hire "hard-to-employ" local residents. Job generation is a critical component in the rebuilding and revitalization of a struggling local economy.
- *Integrate immigrants into the American Dream.* In many areas of the United States, immigrants hold a large percentage of the entry-level service and manufacturing jobs. By employing these new neighbors, you can help integrate immigrants into your local community and support them in achieving the American Dream.
- *Create a culture of community involvement.* You can create a corporate culture that rewards and encourages employees

to get involved in the community and its nonprofit organizations. This could be in the form of involving employees in a corporate giving program, paying staff members for volunteer community work, or including support of a local community project in staff members' job descriptions.

- *Offer employees ownership in the company.* When you offer employees an ownership stake in your company, not only do your employees gain financially, but your company also benefits from the increased staff commitment. The stronger and deeper the connection that employees have to their place of work, the more likely the company will thrive, remain in the community, and participate in community projects and programs. Several forms of employee ownership are available to small and midsized companies, including employee stock ownership plans (ESOPs) and sales of stock.

The paths to partnering with staff members to improve your community are limitless, and the benefits to your business are enormous. For example, the Greyston Bakery is a values-driven company that has developed a groundbreaking system for hiring and training hard-to-employ community residents. Its profound commitment to forging strong and deep partnerships with its employees and its community has been fundamental to its success.

Partnering with Employees:
The Greyston Bakery, Yonkers, New York

The Greyston Bakery was founded in 1982 by a Zen Buddhist community led by a one-time aerospace engineer, Bernard Tetsugen Glassman. Bernie, as he is known, borrowed $300,000 to open a small storefront bakery in the Bronx. The plan was to make enough money to free the Buddhist staff members from their normal jobs so they could have more fulfilling work and more time to meditate. And the plan worked—within a matter of months they were earning their daily bread in a meditative atmosphere, turning out muffins, scones, and cakes for the neighborhood as well as for upscale restaurants in Manhattan.

As the business grew, so did Bernie's vision. He envisioned a community-based business that would marry his spirituality with his belief in service and social action. When the time came to move the bakery in 1985, a vacant pasta factory became available in Yonkers, New York. Yonkers, an inner-city community, was experiencing an economic and cultural decline. Although Yonkers is in Westchester County, one of the richest counties in America, it had the highest per capita population of homeless people in the nation.

Bernie jumped at the chance to move the business to an area that desperately needed some signs of economic life. The move was a major statement to the Yonkers community—it demonstrated faith in the future of Yonkers.

The next milestone for Greyston was a chance encounter (Bernie would say that there are no accidents) between Bernie and the legendary entrepreneur of ice cream, Ben Cohen, at an SVN conference. Ben was looking for ways to leverage his business to save the world, and Bernie was looking for ways to save his business. They quickly found common ground and laid the foundation for a mutually beneficial contract that would put Greyston's brownies inside Ben & Jerry's Ice Cream for many years to come. This partnership gave Greyston the economic stability it sorely needed and pleased millions of ice cream eaters. The partnership continues to be an economic cornerstone and major promotional tool for Greyston.

By 1995 Greyston had established roots in Yonkers and Bernie decided it was time to pass the baton to new leadership.

After a couple of years of temporary CEOs, Julius Walls became the company's fourth CEO in 1997. Julius has proven to be a worthy successor to Bernie and a faithful keeper of the Greyston entrepreneurial spirit and its social mission. Under his leadership, the Greyston Bakery has grown to become a gourmet wholesale-retail bakery whose cakes, pies, and other desserts are sold around the nation, generating more than $5 million in revenues and employing over forty people.

Along with its parent, the nonprofit Greyston Foundation, the bakery has served as a magnet for economic development in Yonkers, helping bring the community back to life. The good works of this business have been featured on *60 Minutes* and in numerous publications. We find the most innovative and compelling Greyston practice to be its revolutionary hiring and training process.

Just doing business in the inner city of Yonkers is a major contribution to the community. According to Greyston's values statement, "The bakery is committed to producing its goods within southwest Yonkers, the community where it was created and has grown, and where there is a high concentration of hard-to-employ individuals. Any expansion elsewhere will only be undertaken if the Yonkers base of operation remains strong."

Greyston's philosophy, as outlined in its values statement, explicitly ties the hiring and training of its staff to its support of the Yonkers community: "The bakery will continue its open-hiring policy, and the associated apprenticeship program, in order to provide opportunity to Yonkers' hard-to-employ population. Providing jobs, and training for those jobs, to individuals who would otherwise likely be unemployed, is one of the greatest benefits that the bakery provides to the community."

The Greyston Bakery's hiring system serves as the gold standard for innovative socially responsible hiring practices. By developing an open hiring system for entry-level employees, the company fulfills its mission to hire and train the hard-to-employ—people who may have poor or no work experience, had been incarcerated, or are former substance abusers. Greyston had the will, and it found a way to hire people based strictly on performance and not on their resumes or interview skills.

The essence of its hiring process is that the first person applying for an entry-level job is hired, period. Here is how it works:

Greyston accepts applications in the order in which they are received. Each applicant is asked to attend a two-hour orientation for ten to twenty people generally beginning at 1:00 p.m. If an applicant shows up at 1:05, he or she is not allowed in but is encouraged to attend the next orientation—showing up on time is a key requirement at Greyston. The orientation describes apprenticeship procedures and the guidelines for employment.

When Greyston has a job opening, the next person in line based on the application date is called and invited to join the apprenticeship program. This on-the-job training is done in a structured and supportive work environment where the apprentice is evaluated on production skills, promptness, attendance, and attitude.

The apprenticeship program is organized into two-week periods. Apprentices who pass eight periods become "permanent" employees, receive full benefits and productivity bonuses, and participate in the profit-sharing program. However, apprentices who fail four periods are asked to leave the program. The expectations are clear and when they are not met, Greyston follows through on the fair and open process it set up. Success is based entirely on performance, not on previous work history.

Since most participants in the apprentice program have had little successful job experience, the program centers on supporting them in getting their lives in order. Greyston recently hired a human resources professional whose only job is to support the apprentices and the staff in not only being better employees but in being happier people.

As might be expected, the apprentice program has a very high turnover rate. In 2005 one in three apprentices completed the eight periods and graduated to permanent employees. According to Julius Walls, "Interestingly, we are not good predictors of who will complete the program and who won't. People who give the best interviews are not always the best employees. We've found on-the-job training and observation is a far superior method for selecting competent staff, especially when compared to the interview and résumé process."

Greyston has a very low turnover rate, with permanent staff members staying at the bakery an average of three years. Of the approximately forty-five current permanent employees, all but six have come through the groundbreaking apprentice program. Julius happily shared that he is now addressing new issues, such as celebrating staff more, including members who have been with the company five years; graduating the apprenticeship; helping employees complete outside education; and implementing a new program, Catch Someone Doing Right, which celebrates the superior work of an employee.

It's important to note that Greyston does not necessarily view turnover as bad. It measures two types of turnover. Positive turnover occurs when a staff member leaves for a better life—for example, a better job or a job closer to home. Negative turnover occurs when the person is asked to leave because of performance issues, such as a negative attitude, poor attendance, or an inability to get the job done. The company doesn't want negative turnover, and the management is on the constant lookout for inventive ways to provide better support for the staff.

Greyston feels positive turnover is good. For example, Rodney Johnson, the former production manager, is just one of many success stories. When he was nineteen, Rodney was hired by Greyston—for his first legitimate job—at an entry-level position. He gave up making thousands of dollars a week by selling drugs for a job netting him a few hundred dollars a week. But Rodney wanted to be a positive role model for his children and show them that there was something better in life. After ten years with the company, Rodney, a father of eight, recently left Greyston to start his own maintenance and cleaning business.

When Expanding a Business, Add Expertise

Greyston has had its share of financial ups and downs and has contantly struggled to be financially sustainable, so the management is always looking for ways to increase profitability. A few years ago it became clear that Greyston needed to expand its operations and build a new bakery. This was a good decision, but as you will see, the way Greyston went about it posed some serious challenges.

Greyston recently designed and built from scratch a $10 million state-of-the art bakery, tripling its capacity. When asked about Greyston's biggest mistake, Julius was quick to single out a miscalculation that Greyston spent months scrambling to address. In his words, "We underestimated the management experience and technological skills necessary to move from a 12,000-square-foot basic manufacturing facility to a fully automated 23,000-square-foot plant."

The reason for building a new high-tech bakery was to expand capacity and to incorporate the technological advances necessary to become more competitive. However, the construction took a year longer than projected and was almost $1 million overbudget. In addition, the construction process drained management energy and hindered Greyston's ability to meet growing customer demand.

Because the project was overbudget, the bakery was forced to shut down the production line in the old bakery and start up the new bakery on the same day, a real trial by fire. The original plan was to run both simultaneously for two weeks to work out the kinks.

This hurried transition didn't give the staff nearly enough time to learn how to use the new equipment and to develop the systems to ensure efficient and quality production. Julius came to the painful realization that the management and staff didn't have either the technological skills or the experience necessary to make this new facility and new equipment work properly. As Julius said, "Our staff was not properly trained, the equipment didn't work, and we had no money. But other than that, everything was fine."

With modern equipment, hands-on adjustments are more difficult to make and there is less room for error. You can't just open the oven door and stick a toothpick in a cake to test if it's done. Once a cake is in the baking tunnel, the settings had better be right or at the end of the line you'll have one of two undesirable results—toast or pudding. Greyston resolved these problems by hiring people with the necessary experience with this high-tech equipment. After almost two years, production is moving smoothly, and Greyston continues its quest to refine the baking systems and increase efficiency.

Balancing the Need for Technology with the Mission of Providing Jobs

Just as engineering a smooth transition from an old, smaller manufacturing plant to a new, larger plant presents challenges, balancing loyalty to staff with production efficiency creates serious complications. How Greyston handled this management tension offers important lessons no matter what your business.

As a manufacturing business, Greyston must keep up-to-date with the latest technology in order to remain competitive. The company also feels an obligation to train bakery employees in advanced skills that will have enduring value in the job market.

The modern bakery enabled Greyston to decrease its number of employees without layoffs (through natural attrition) from sixty-five in early 2004 to forty-five by 2005. The more efficient manufacturing process resulted in increased profitability, which is necessary for Greyston to achieve one of its most important objectives—paying all employees a living wage. A living wage for a family of four in Yonkers is currently $10.50 an hour plus benefits. Greyston starts entry-level workers at $7.00 per hour with benefits that include sick time, vacation pay, and fully paid medical insurance.

However, another cornerstone of Greyston's mission is to provide jobs, hopefully a growing number of jobs, for hard-to-employ community residents. This presents a conundrum for a values-driven company. How can Greyston remain competitive while continuing to provide a growing (or at least stable) number of jobs?

Greyston's solution to this management tension has been to run a successful business: automate the bakery and simultaneously grow the business by introducing new products and ramping up marketing. And the plan is starting to work! Revenues increased from $4.8 million in 2004 to $5.3 million in 2006—and as of this writing the number of staff is forty-five people. Through its recent upgrade in technology and its current rate of growth, Greyston has successfully addressed a management challenge and is one step closer to paying all of its workers a living wage.

Greyston has developed a successful model for advancing the careers and improving the lives of employees that is inspirational and instructive. For Julius, building business-staff partnerships is a work in progress requiring daily attention. And he sees the benefits to his business and his community derived from these vital partnerships every day.

Best Practices in Partnering with Employees

Like Greyston Bakery, Zingerman's Delicatessen in Ann Arbor, Michigan, grasps the critical importance of business-staff partnerships and has developed its own unique way of supporting the growth and development of its staff.

Building New Business:
Zingerman's Delicatessen, Ann Arbor, Michigan

Paul Saginaw and Ari Weinzweig opened Zingerman's Delicatessen in March 1982 in a historic building near the Ann Arbor Farmers' Market. It began with a limited menu of specialty foods, traditional Jewish dishes, and sandwiches and grew to become one of Ann Arbor's most popular restaurants and retail businesses. And Zingerman's goes beyond the food by aiming to present it in an entertaining, educational, and service-oriented setting. *Inc.* magazine called Zingerman's the Coolest Small Company in America, and you'll soon see why.[7]

Great food and good fun have been the engine for Zingerman's growth. However, instead of opening more delis or even a Zingerman's chain, Paul and Ari chose to grow into other food-related businesses (what traditionally would be called vertical growth). Zingerman's is now a community of seven businesses—a delicatessen; a full-service, sit-down restaurant featuring regional American food; a catering business; a bakery; a coffee company; a cheese-making company; and a training and consulting business. The Zingerman's community of businesses has become a highly effective system for partnering with employees and turning many of them into managers and even owners. Each business has at least one managing partner on site, and the community has fifteen partners with 400 employees and generates $29 million in revenues.

This growth strategy fits nicely into Zingerman's mission of providing well-paying and fulfilling jobs to people in the community. The plan is to grow in a relatively slow and sustainable way that enables Zingerman's to hire new employees while giving staff members opportunities to develop their careers. Zingerman's long-term objective is to start one or two businesses a year, resulting in twelve to fifteen food-related companies by 2009, all located in the Ann Arbor area.

The leaders of Zingerman's operate as partners with their staff members and highly value employee participation and full engagement of staff. They know the business needs full buy-in by employees, and they are consistent in their message that every member must take responsibility for business success. These innovative leaders also know that management cannot ask for employee responsibility without providing complete company information and including staff in the decision-making process. At Zingerman's, employee empowerment is not just a buzzword; it's an integral part of the company culture.

The community of businesses is managed by a partners group that meets twice a month and includes fifteen owners and executive officers. The meetings are open to all staff members, and all finances are open too. The partners make great efforts to create a culture where everyone's ideas are heard and seriously considered. Employees are asked to participate in decisions affecting them, and decisions are made based on what is the best solution for the whole community.

Training programs are a critical part of the Zingerman's culture, and classes clarify the company's mission and reason for existence and emphasize the principles that guide what Zingerman's does. Every employee is required to take a class on open-book management, which teaches how the business works and how to read profit and loss statements and balance sheets. All partners teach classes and are involved in other aspects of staff training. The superior training given to Zingerman's employees not only helps staff members advance within the company but gives them skills to make career changes outside the company as well.

As the reputation of Zingerman's legendary customer service grew, other businesses became interested in how the company did it. So it started Zing Train, a new business that trains the managers and employees of other businesses. Building partnerships with employees and creating entrepreneurs inside and outside the Zingerman's community of companies has become one of its many trademark practices. In fact, twelve of the fifteen owners came up through the business.

Zingerman's staff guide is an impressive and colorful handbook outlining the company's vision and guiding principles and specific ways to share the Zingerman's experience. On page 1 is the Zingerman's Mission Statement:

> We share the Zingerman's experience
> selling food that makes you happy
> giving service that makes you smile
> in passionate pursuit of our mission
> showing love and caring in all our actions
> to enrich as many lives as we possibly can.

Zingerman's donates 10 percent of profits to community nonprofits, and each Zingerman's business also contributes substantial in-kind donations. In 1988 Paul, with the help of Zingerman's, founded Food Gatherers, a food rescue program that collects leftover food from local restaurants and distributes it to the hungry.

Zingerman's also played a major role in the development of the Delonis Center, a collaboration between a number of organizations in Ann Arbor to feed and shelter the homeless. Now housed in a brand new building, it teaches homeless people how to cook and prepare food for other homeless people.

While Zingerman's has chosen to expand its business by growing new businesses connected to its core business, a small construction company on an island off the coast of Massachusetts has found a way to partner with staff members by bringing them into the ownership of the company.

Creating an Employee-Owned Company:
South Mountain Company, Martha's Vineyard, Massachusetts

South Mountain Company is an employee-owned design-build firm that constructs and renovates houses of all types—large and small, affordable and very high end, new and old—and even whole neighborhoods. The founder and CEO, John Abrams, wonders why more companies that consider themselves to be socially responsible or values-driven do not embrace employee ownership as part of their missions.

In his book, *The Company We Keep: Reinventing Small Business for People, Community, and Place,* John stresses the importance of partnerships: "We not only build houses, we build connections and bonds between people, between people and land, and between commerce and place."[8] South Mountain Company stands out as a great example of how a small business partners with employees by including them in the ownership, resulting in a stronger business more deeply connected to the community.

Like so many companies, South Mountain began as a family business. As the company grew, its informal, more intuitive approach to doing business needed to change. Two of John's key, longtime employees came to him and said they wanted to stay at South Mountain, but they needed a greater stake in the company and something more than hourly wages. This request led to an extended inquiry into how South Mountain should be structured to ensure its long-term success and stability. John and his staff members concluded that the new structure should ensure that anyone making a career at South Mountain could enjoy the financial rewards as well as the headaches that come from owning a business.

An attorney from the Industrial Cooperatives Association (now known as the ICA Group) began laying out specific legal and structural options. During this time, John came face to face with some very tough issues. If he lost control of the company, what would happen if he got outvoted and the company moved down a path he thought would bring financial or mission-related disaster? John came to realize that for the company to achieve its mission, he would have to take this leap of faith and include others as owner-partners in the business. So he made the jump, and South Mountain adopted a democratic ownership structure modeled after the Mondragon worker-owned cooperatives in the Basque area of Spain.

One of the major safeguards in the new structure was the requirement that before someone became an owner, he or she would have to work for South Mountain for at least five years. This ensured that the current owners had time to assess the individual and gave the employee enough time to learn about the company and understand all that was required for ownership. In addition, an ownership entry fee was set that was significant but not so high that it would discourage good people from joining.

On January 1, 1987, John transferred ownership to a new worker-owned cooperative corporation. Almost twenty years later, how is South Mountain doing? The sixteen owners (only one owner has left during the previous decade) feel the company is operating at its optimum volume of business, and they share 35 percent of the profits every year. All of the thirty-two employees are paid a living wage, and the company pays 100 percent of the best available health insurance package, including dental and alternative health care. South Mountain also offers paternity and maternity leave, a pension plan, a profit-sharing program, and flexibility to take time off when needed.

John has found that as the ownership group expands, a wider diversity of viewpoints is expressed and thus more disagreements occur. However, this has been an advantage, creating richer discussions and more thoughtful decisions. It has also required more artful facilitation of meetings and a conscious effort to balance efficiency with participation. The hierarchy of South Mountain is based more on expertise than on percentage of ownership. John has continued to be the leader and CEO, and he is the public voice of the company and its primary salesperson, but even that is beginning to change.

From the very beginning, being involved in the community was a matter of course for the company and for the staff. The company supports its staff in playing a role in local government, and employees have held many committee positions, including positions on housing commissions, on regional planning agencies, and even as commissioner. Staff members have been involved in a variety of community efforts to promote sustainability and create desperately needed affordable housing. They are free to do what is necessary to pursue their community work, even if it means time off in the middle of the day.

John Abrams takes a long-range view of South Mountain Company: "We recognize that any wealth that has accrued to us has been provided in significant measure from the capital of this community, and it is our obligation to ensure that our business becomes an enduring part of the fabric of this community. To make a durable, robust, and flexible business community that outlasts its original owners, we plan for succession so that as we age we can gracefully depart and leave the company—vibrant, stable, learning—in the hands of others." Whereas John structured his business so that it encourages employees to become owners of the company they work for, Jim Kelly devised an employee program that encourages ownership of a different sort: homeownership.

Supporting Employees in Becoming Homeowners: Rejuvenation, Portland, Oregon

Rejuvenation manufactures and markets reproduction lighting and house parts. You'll find its products in homes and commercial and public buildings throughout the United States, including Grand Central Station and Hearst Castle. The company has a very diverse workforce, with fourteen countries represented among the 250 employees, 80 percent of whom are paid hourly wages.

Founder and owner Jim Kelly felt it was wrong that Rejuvenation helped customers beautify their homes but many of its employees would never be able to afford to own a house. He had just joined the local housing authority board and learned that not having money for a down payment was a crucial hurdle for the working poor. Jim decided to do something about it.

He came up with a straightforward program to encourage homeownership—the Home Buying Program. Rejuvenation would pay a $5,000 down payment on an employee's first home, which could not cost more than a set price. If the employee remained with the company for five years, the loan was forgiven.

To Jim's disappointment, no one used the program in the first few years. The Portland real estate market was hot, and few houses were available at the maximum price set. A change in the program was needed: the maximum cost of a house was set at 90 percent of the median house value. Now there were some takers!

However, some employees bought new houses in the suburbs, far away from the factory, resulting in long commutes. That did not fit well with the company's ambition to be an environmental leader. Another adjustment was necessary: a provision was added that the home had to be at least thirty-five years old. Older homes were closer to the factory, making it possible to commute by bus. The employees could now also buy reproduction house parts from Rejuvenation to upgrade their new homes.

Jim is understandably proud of the fact that the company has helped ten employees build equity of about $1 million because housing prices have increased substantially in the past eight years. These new homeowners are now more established in the community—the Home Buying Program has truly made a difference for them.

Lessons Learned: Partnering with Employees

There is no limit to the ways a business can grow local value by supporting staff members and involving them in the business. The work of the entrepreneurs featured in this chapter offers us several important lessons:

- **Create jobs.** We cannot overstate the importance of job creation. One of the most important benefits you can provide your community and the local economy is a business that offers well-paying and satisfying jobs to local residents.
- **Hire the hard-to-employ.** Hiring and training the hard-to-employ is challenging and yet very rewarding work. To do it effectively, you need to develop a systematic hiring process and apprentice program that offers a wide range of support services.
- **Balance high-tech with "high-touch" when making technological upgrades.** The need to remain competitive technologically can be balanced with the desire to remain loyal to

your staff. Do everything possible to prevent layoffs, including finding new ways to grow the business or simply being patient and letting natural attrition take its course. When a company successfully prevents layoffs during tough times or business transitions, employee loyalty and performance soar.

- **Help employees attain the American Dream.** Your business can make a life-changing impact on employees by offering a program that encourages them to become homeowners. When you help immigrants or low-income staff members get their financial feet on the ground and purchase their first home, you help create a more stable team of employees and a more diverse and inclusive community.

- **Realize that there's more than one way to grow a company.** You can grow your company and expand the careers of your staff members without creating a chain or a franchise. Building a community of related businesses that leverages the strengths of your core business can be a way of expanding management and ownership opportunities within the business as well as increasing profits.

- **Consider employee ownership.** Bringing employees into the ownership of your company is an excellent way to reward and retain loyal employees. When staff members become actual owners of the business, they have more at stake and become more committed. This results in a stronger company and a stronger community.

Have you attended seminars and conferences focusing on how to motivate staff and develop a powerful team of associates? Well, we've found that one of the best ways to gain full engagement from staff members is to work with them to improve themselves and their community. This chapter offers merely a taste of the literally hundreds of examples of the imaginative ways small companies partner with employees to grow local value. In chapter 4 we'll explore a relatively new way of making a difference in the community: partnering with your fellow entrepreneurs.

4

Business networking for local value

It's likely that one reason you've chosen to become an entrepreneur is to be free and independent, but when you open a business, you're actually joining a network of literally thousands of interdependent businesses. Not only are the partnerships we form within this network critical to our success and the longevity of our businesses, but they also present tremendous opportunities to grow local value.

The three basic categories of businesses that you can form partnerships with are businesses traditionally referred to as vendors or suppliers, businesses in your industry, and local businesses in your community.

If you run a grocery store, hardware store, or other retail establishment, you are dependent on the companies that supply you with the products you sell. If you are a manufacturer, you rely on suppliers, distributors, and retailers. Even if you own a software company, you require the support of companies that construct computers as well as those that market and package your product.

In some companies the relationships with vendors are perhaps less obvious, but no less important, and include insurance agents, HMOs, and janitorial services. When these relationships work, your business can focus its time and energy on upgrading existing products, creating new products, and improving customer service. When these relationships don't work, doing business can be problematic. In extreme cases, poor vendor relationships can actually bring down a business. For example, a poor relationship with an insurance agent can mean not having an appropriate policy when dealing with the aftermath of a hurricane.

Those of us who have been in business for a while generally sing the praises of our vendors and suppliers. In fact, a special relationship with a vendor can become a unique selling proposition, such as Hanna Andersson's Swedish manufacturer supplying high-quality children's clothing not previously available anywhere in the United States. Similarly, positive relationships with local businesses and other companies in the same industry can grow local value and greatly benefit the community. But what is often underrated is that when you have well-oiled working relationships with other businesses, you'll find surprising and significant ways to collaborate that greatly benefit the financial strength of your business.

Building strong relationships with fellow entrepreneurs means treating the people you do business with fairly and ethically. Paying bills on time, following through on contracts, respecting competitors, and keeping lines of communication open are all part of building a strong network of supportive businesses. These solid business practices also help cultivate a local economy based on honesty and trust. And when this is the way you do business, your company will receive abundant short-term and long-term financial benefits. Ethical business practices are a terrific example of how the expression "what goes around, comes around" actually works. And the vendor-boomerang effect shows itself almost immediately.

Here are five ways you can partner with other businesses to strengthen your company and your community:

- *Be a loyal business partner and place a financial value on vendor relationships.* Going beyond fair business practices and making the effort to build strong bonds with vendors and suppliers can have a profound impact on your business. Vendors are often local entrepreneurs just like you, who live or die based on a series of relationships with other businesses. In fact, it's not unusual for a vendor's success to be tied to a few major contracts. The Golden Rule applies— "Do unto others as you would have them do unto you."

Shortsightedly, some entrepreneurs make decisions concerning vendors and suppliers based on price alone, but the lowest price could include hidden costs. In addition, a long and strong relationship with a business partner can have many measurable benefits beyond price, such as the ability to respond to your changing needs, prompt service, and product quality and consistency. The Longfellow Clubs has a general rule that it will stick with a long-standing and successful business partnership unless a new vendor's bid is at least 15 to 20 percent lower. Even then, the current vendor will be given a chance to sharpen its pencils in a cooperative effort to maintain the relationship.

Of course, all contracts with business partners should be evaluated periodically to see if they still best serve your business. However, the process of choosing or switching vendors should be transparent to all involved parties, and your company should place a dollar amount on the time, trust, and risk involved in moving to a new business relationship. When you develop a network of solid and mutually beneficial business partnerships, you are growing local value as the community benefits from the mutually strengthened companies.

- *Expand your business partnerships to include women and entrepreneurs of color.* As an entrepreneur, you have major opportunities to help address the issue of fairness and economic justice in our world. One relatively easy way is to do business with companies that are owned and managed by women and people of color. You may need to do some work to find companies that meet your needs and are owned by women or people of color, but making the effort to have a more diverse set of business relationships is good for your business, good for the vendors, and good for the harmony and equity in the community.

- *Leverage your business to influence a vendor's practices and help build other values-driven businesses.* SVN member and Ben & Jerry's cofounder Ben Cohen has been a pioneer in leveraging his company's purchasing power to make a contribution to the community. He went to extraordinary lengths to make the business partnership with the Greyston Bakery work for both parties, and the result was a mutually profitable relationship that has lasted for years. Whether you choose vendors that are already partnering with the community or influence companies to do more, your vendor relationships can go a long way to growing local value.

- *Collaborate with fellow business owners in your industry and support your trade association.* Small business owners are finding great value in getting together for mutual support. Trade associations have become an important phenomenon in the evolution of modern-day business. Many of these associations have progressed beyond the largely bygone era when "good old boys" got together to party, make anticompetitive deals, and scheme to influence regressive legislation (fighting minimum wage increases, for example).

Today many trade associations systematically share information that helps entrepreneurs, and ultimately the industry as a whole, by introducing technological advancements and sharing best practices.

Cooperation among businesses in the same industry/sector can be a major factor in business success. The more effective and advanced the trade association, the easier it is for companies to adapt to changing times. Entrepreneurial competition becomes more of a friendly challenge than a threat as businesses work as partners to improve and promote their industry. And many progressive business associations also emphasize community service and encourage entrepreneurs to find ways to grow their businesses by being good community citizens. They've found that growing local value is good for business.

- *Join with other independent, locally owned businesses and start a Local First campaign.* For the past twenty years, independent, locally owned businesses have been under a sustained assault from chains and big-box stores owned by mammoth multinational companies. These retail giants rarely create new demand: they generally siphon off business from existing retailers. The result is boarded up Main Streets and a very unfriendly climate for small local retailers.

A growing movement in North America is composed of business networks promoting purchasing from locally owned, independent businesses. Campaigns currently exist in over thirty communities, including Bellingham, Washington; Salt Lake City, Utah; Chicago, Illinois; Portland, Oregon; and Cambridge, Massachusetts. These collaborative efforts are changing the way customers think about their purchasing choices. They are learning that where they spend their shopping dollars can be a vote that is as important as a ballot cast on election day. By making even small modifications in the buying habits of just a small portion of customers, these campaigns have increased local sales and improved the climate for doing business as an independent.

The potential for business-to-business partnerships to grow local value is immense. Judy Wicks did what she needed to do to grow her values-driven business and in the process expanded the businesses of local farmers and helped create a new local, cruelty-free food system.

Partnering with Other Businesses:
The White Dog Cafe, Philadelphia, Pennsylvania

Judy Wicks, founder of the White Dog Cafe, has committed her life to helping build an economically just and environmentally sustainable world. She sees her business as a player in a myriad of networks that shape our economy, and she seeks to use her entrepreneurial influence to lift up the common good.

Judy understands at a gut level the importance of positive relationships with other local entrepreneurs. For her, it comes naturally; it's a part of who she is. She cares about the people in her life and she has a deep desire to build harmony in her world. Building strong relationships and empowering all the stakeholders of the White Dog Cafe is embedded in its mission and manifested through it values and practices.

The White Dog Cafe opened for business in 1983 as a takeout coffee and muffin shop on the first floor of Judy's house. The menu soon expanded to include soup and sandwiches. By 1989 the White Dog had grown to a full-service restaurant, seating over 200 customers, and the adjacent Black Cat Gift Shop had opened its doors.

A turning point in Judy's life came when she, on Ben Cohen's suggestion, attended her first SVN conference. She reveled in this newly found community of businesses that shared her values and aimed to change the world. SVN also provided a platform for Judy's work, and she soon became one of its most visible leaders, serving as chair of SVN.

One day Judy was listening to a tape of a book by John Robbins (the heir to the Baskin-Robbins chain), *Diet for a New America.* Judy was horrified when she learned about the barbarous way hogs were raised and slaughtered. She knew that she could no longer be a party to this cruel system. She had to do something, but what? Should she become a vegetarian? Should she eliminate meat from the menu?

One morning after several sleepless nights, she walked into the White Dog Cafe kitchen and told her staff that she could no longer participate in a system based on cruelty toward animals. Judy and her chef decided that since people probably wouldn't give up eating meat anytime soon, the White Dog would continue to offer meat as a culinary choice along with an expanded selection of vegetarian dishes. But they agreed that all White Dog animal products would be purchased from farms that raised and slaughtered animals in a humane way. They took pork off the menu until they could find humanely raised pork to replace it. The chef staff soon learned that the local supplier of their free-range chickens also raised pigs humanely. These hogs were raised in a meadow with enough space to move around, bred naturally, and slaughtered humanely. The chef proceeded to order two pasture-raised pigs a week.

As it turned out, this soul-searching process led to another value-added ingredient in Judy's business recipe. She had created a market niche for the White Dog Cafe by offering a cruelty-free menu, which gave it a competitive edge over other restaurants in Philadelphia.

But Judy wasn't finished yet. The more she became involved in the issue of humanely grown meat, the more she realized that if she really wanted to support local farmers, get people to eat humanely grown hogs, and support an alternative to factory farming, she needed to create more demand and encourage other restaurants to join her in purchasing from these local farmers.

To be true to her values she moved from making this a niche for her restaurant to working to broaden this practice and inviting other restaurants to join her in serving pasture-raised meat. She began spreading the gospel and soon many local restaurateurs jumped on board, resulting in a sizeable increase in demand for humanely raised pork.

By partnering with local farmers and other restaurant owners, Judy had helped engineer an increase in the demand, but now a new problem arose—the supply of humanely grown pork could not keep up with the growing demand. Judy asked the hog farmer who supplied her with meat if he wanted to expand his business. He was enthusiastic but told her he couldn't handle the growth without a refrigerated truck. So Judy raised the stakes of her partnership with this supplier: she offered to lend the farmer $30,000 at 5 percent interest to buy a new refrigerated truck to deliver meat to restaurants all over Philadelphia. He took her up on this offer and expanded his business.

Judy was learning about local food systems through first-hand experience. By building strong vendor relationships she had created a solution to her restaurant's (and neighboring restaurants') need to serve humanely raised meat, but Judy began thinking bigger. She became active in the national movement to support local hog farming that provides an important alternative to the factory farms that pollute the environment and house tens of thousands of hogs in crowded and inhumane conditions.

Eastern Pennsylvania needed an alternative food system that could grow substantial amounts of humanely raised meat, distribute it efficiently, and ensure enough customer demand to make the whole system work economically. So Judy created the

White Dog Cafe Foundation, which is funded from 20 percent of the profits of the White Dog Cafe. The first program of the foundation was the Fair Food Project, focusing on building a humane and sustainable local food system.

The foundation then set up the Pig Farmer's Assistance Project and in collaboration with another foundation awarded $10,000 grants to four pig farmers. The grants were used to expand the pasture-raised, hormone-free pork business. Judy knows the success of her business and the vibrancy of her local economy are directly tied to the success of her business partners.

Judy recognized that it isn't enough to make your own company more socially responsible. Business leaders need to partner with a network of businesses that collectively contribute to building strong local living economies. This understanding played an important role in the establishment of a group Judy and Laury cofounded in 2001—the Business Alliance for Local Living Economies (BALLE). This international network of local business networks throughout North America has become a leader in supporting the growth of values-driven businesses.

Judy also founded a local BALLE network, the Sustainable Business Network of Philadelphia (SBN). SBN is a pioneer in organizing businesses around the building blocks of a strong local living economy—food, energy, clothing, shelter, retailing, and so on. By offering educational programs and networking opportunities for local businesses, SBN is strengthening member companies and helping build a strong Philadelphia economy. Recently, SBN initiated a leading Local First campaign that encouraged citizens to buy from local merchants and to support local agriculture.

Don't Order Your Chickens until the Financing Hatches

Not every relationship with vendors has been so seamless for Judy. Like all of us, she's made her fair share of business gaffes.

One memorable miscalculation presented serious problems for Judy and her vendors, but the lessons she learned from this error have stuck with her and made her a better entrepreneur.

When asked about her biggest business mistake, Judy is quick to recount the problems she encountered when she opened the Black Cat Gift Shop in 1989. As is her style, she approached this new entrepreneurial adventure with great gusto. Assuming financing would be secured, she placed orders with vendors so she would have a fully stocked store on opening day. But the financing took longer than anticipated, and she was forced to ship some orders back and cancel many others.

This was quite stressful and embarrassing for Judy since she was dealing with many small businesses and craftspeople who were counting on her. When she realized the financing was going to be late, she immediately contacted her vendors and explained the situation. Because of her solid reputation and the trust she had developed, they worked with her. When the financing finally came through, she reordered everything. As a result of Judy's honesty and forthrightness, the Black Cat eventually became a valued long-term business partner with many of these vendors, helping it become a profitable part of her business.

As you can see, Judy places great importance on relationships. She always endeavors to work with vendors who share her values and to be a good business partner with the businesses and farmers who supply her restaurant. But it's not always easy.

Balancing Buying from Local Farmers with Maintaining Consistency and Efficiency

A major component of the White Dog Cafe's mission is to support local agriculture. The White Dog goes to great lengths to buy locally grown organic produce whenever possible, and it advertises this fact on the menu.

However, major challenges arise when you decide to "go local and organic" because you're working with an emerging food system that is not fully developed. The White Dog staff must make extra efforts to order food based on when it is ready to harvest, deal with multiple suppliers and distributors, and be prepared to learn at the last minute that an order can't be filled exactly as it was made. What happens if you don't need as many vegetables as the farmer brings to your door because he had so many ready to be harvested? Do you buy it all and possibly lose money on the deal? What happens if you run out of local pasture-raised pork? Do you supplement it with pork shipped in long distance? These are difficult questions with no easy answers. The need to provide consistency in the menu and support the cafe staff sometimes conflicts with the sustainable mission of the White Dog.

Judy's solution to this management tension is to acknowledge the challenges of working locally and organically and to plan accordingly. This means setting up systems, having backup plans, and offering support to those responsible for ordering food and working with vendors. These extraordinary efforts have helped build the White Dog's reputation as a restaurant committed to local agriculture and as a caring member of the community.

Judy is fully aware of the current fast-food mentality of wanting what we want and wanting it now. However, she understands that nature and sustainable agriculture cannot be treated like a mechanized factory. Sustainable farming involves real plants and real animals that need to be treated with respect and that require great patience. Judy's very sympathetic to the "slow-food movement," where the emphasis is on quality, authentic taste, and a pleasurable experience.

Best Practices in Partnering with Other Businesses

On the opposite side of the country from the White Dog, an Oregon values-driven restaurateur has a mission similar to Judy's but took a different approach. The result has been equally remarkable.

Promoting Local Agriculture:
Higgins Restaurant, Portland, Oregon

As an avid bicyclist, Greg Higgins enjoyed his long and winding rides along the farmlands in Oregon's Willamette Valley during the 1980s. He took pleasure in the looks on farmers' faces as he stopped to introduce himself and talk about his desire for an increased supply of locally grown ingredients at the popular hotel restaurant where he was the head chef.

When Greg opened his own high-end restaurant, Higgins, in downtown Portland in 1994, he was carrying out his longtime vision—a restaurant featuring locally grown organic foods and a menu that shifted with the seasons. Although his innovative menu received rave reviews from connoisseurs, the early years were not without their challenges. A restaurant limiting its offerings to foods that were locally in season was a new concept and left some customers wanting favorite, familiar ingredients. And while Greg had developed a fairly extensive network of local farmers, he could not always find suitable quantities of certain seasonal ingredients. With few restaurants in the area focused on buying locally, farmers could not afford to grow crops based on the needs of just a few high-end restaurants.

In an attempt to increase his access to the foods he wanted, he encouraged other chefs to join him in promoting local agriculture by establishing the Portland chapter of the national Chefs Collaborative. The collaborative works with chefs and the food community to celebrate local foods and foster a more sustainable food supply. It also educates people as to the importance of supporting community farmers. This support keeps local economies strong by increasing jobs and helps conserve fossil fuels by reducing the need for food to make long, refrigerated journeys.

Under Greg's leadership, the Portland Chefs Collaborative set out to create a platform for connecting farmers and chefs. Through annual Farmer-Chef Connection conferences, the collaborative provides opportunities for farmers, fishermen, and chefs to come together and build relationships while learning about new products and talking about how to work together effectively. Its Web site serves as a business-to-business marketing tool, allowing farmers to list available products or search for chefs in need of specific products and vice versa. It boasts listings from over 200 farmers and fishermen and nearly 250 restaurant buyers in the Pacific Northwest, and the list continues to grow. The annual conferences, which started with sixty attendees, now turn away prospects once registration reaches 300.

With a greater demand for local products, the number of local farms working directly with restaurants has increased. Farmers are eager to talk with Greg about what he hopes to buy in upcoming seasons so they can plan accordingly. As a result, Greg is able to buy 85 percent of his products locally, making exceptions only for essentials that are not produced or grown in Oregon, such as olive oil and coffee. With locally focused restaurants on the rise, Higgins's customers are also more educated on local values and more accepting of seasonal menus. Whereas Greg used to get complaints about not providing tomatoes on sandwiches in January, he now has a loyal following that patiently awaits the return of certain menu items each season.

By educating others in his industry about the importance of buying locally, Greg was ultimately able to increase the supply of products and his own access to them. Customers are drawn by Higgins's commitment to local farmers. Annual sales are nearly $4 million, and the ever-changing menu, which Greg refers to as "creativity controlled by climate," has twice claimed the Restaurant of the Year title from the *Oregonian* newspaper. Greg feels he's succeeded at more than the restaurant business—he's supporting the local economy and environment and helping make Oregonians more aware of their community.

But entrepreneurs in the food business aren't the only ones who are partnering with vendors and other businesses to grow local value. In the inner city of Boston, Beth Williams leveraged her relationships with other businesses to build a new and profitable manufacturing business that created jobs for local residents.

Building an Inner-City Business:
Roxbury Technology Corporation, Boston, Massachusetts

Beth Williams was a single mother working at Blue Cross Blue Shield of Massachusetts when her father, Archie Williams, suddenly died of a stroke. He was the dearly beloved rock of the family, and this unexpected trauma shook the Williams family to the core.

After the initial stages of grieving, the family was confronted with what to do with the young business Archie had recently started—Roxbury Technology Corporation (RTC) based in an inner-city community in Boston. RTC was a distributor of recycled toner cartridges that were primarily sold to Staples, the Boston-based multibillion-dollar chain of large stationery stores.

When Archie died, RTC was two years old and just beginning to get some traction, and Beth felt compelled to honor her father's legacy. Equally important, she lived in Roxbury and was passionate about her community and committed to building a strong local economy in the inner city of Boston. Although she had no previous entrepreneurial experience, she took the plunge, quitting her job and becoming the CEO of RTC.

Like so many entrepreneurs, she had no real idea what this decision was going to mean to her life. Suddenly she was trying to read balance sheets, look for refinancing, deal with partner businesses, and work with the high standards and demands of her primary customer. It was overwhelming, but she was committed to the two-part company mission of strengthening her inner-city community and helping preserve the environment. Hers is a story of how a resourceful entrepreneur successfully leveraged the mission of her company to build partnerships with other businesses.

One of her first efforts was to ask for help from the leading venture capitalist in Boston who specializes in funding African-American businesses—Ed Dugger of UNC Partners. He helped her navigate some stormy entrepreneurial waters and introduced her to other business leaders in the community who bought into her vision.

The next challenge was to develop a strategic plan that would take RTC into the future as a strong player in the highly competitive field of recycled toner cartridges. At first RTC was solely a distributor of cartridges remanufactured by others. She knew that for RTC to be independent and to grow strong roots, it would need to have its own remanufacturing plant. Moving into remanufacturing became pivotal to RTC's future.

After a series of complicated negotiations, Beth was able to form a partnership with one of her potential vendors. This company was an out-of-state toner cartridge remanufacturer that in exchange for future business agreed to help her set up a new toner remanufacturing plant and train her staff. She then was able to identify a location for a new plant in close proximity to a large pool of employable inner-city residents. The space was owned by the Pine Street Inn, a nonprofit enterprise that served the homeless of Boston. Beth signed a lease that was good for both parties and had an ideal location with a fair annual rent.

She then needed to find financing for the expansion. RTC had relatively small debt and an invaluable business partner in Staples, but she was quickly turned down by the two largest banks in New England. Fortunately Sovereign Bank, a regional bank with a former connection to her dad and to Staples, Sovereign Bank offered her an excellent financing package. With everything in place, Beth, utilizing her variety of business partnerships, did the build-out, hired staff, and brought the new inner-city remanufacturing plant into reality.

One August morning in 2004, with great pomp and circumstance, RTC had its grand opening with all the local dignitaries, the governor of Massachusetts, the bankers, and the leaders of Staples, including founder Tom Stemberg. It was a great moment for RTC, for the inner city of Boston, and for the memory of Archie Williams. In 2005 RTC had generated $11.5 million in revenues and is projected to do $14 million in 2006. Beth's manufacturing plant continues to increase its volume and she now employs thirty people from the local community.

Lessons Learned: Partnering with Other Businesses

Following are some of the lessons the entrepreneurs highlighted in this chapter have learned about partnering with fellow businesses:

- **Cultivate strong business.** When you start a business, you soon learn that all businesses face the ups and downs of cash flow—it's part of the deal. If you communicate honestly and on a timely basis, vendors will empathize and work with you when cash is tight. The stronger your relationships are with fellow entrepreneurs, the better they will serve and support your business.

- **Seek sound advice and solid counsel.** Many entrepreneurs are happy to offer suggestions and support to new entrepreneurs. They remember their roots and how tough it was for them in the early years. The prime candidates are entrepreneurs in your local community, leaders in your industry, and friends who know you and believe in you. The guidance can be powerful, and their business connections may end up being even more significant.

- **Make a strategic partnership with a key customer or vendor.** In the beginning, developing a special relationship with an important customer or vendor can help you put your business on a sound financial footing. However, over time it's important to develop a diversified customer base so you can remain independent and not be at the mercy of one customer or vendor.

- **Buy local first.** Buying from local and independent businesses and farms has trade-offs. It may require time and patience, and the process isn't always as predictable as working with a national supplier. You may even need to work with other businesses to help develop a new local supply chain. It may take a bit more work; however, in the long run, not only does doing business with local vendors help build a strong local economy, but it can present a competitive advantage for your business.

- **Join the movement.** Consider starting a Local First campaign with other businesses in your community to educate your customers, other businesses, and the government about the importance of buying locally. This campaign can help local businesses survive and thrive, strengthen the local economy, and preserve the character of your community.

As you've seen, pioneering entrepreneurs are paving new roads for partnering with other businesses to grow local value. No doubt about it, business partnerships are the wave of the future. In a similar vein, leading-edge business leaders are finding groundbreaking pathways for partnering with nonprofits. The new business-nonprofit partnerships examined in the next chapter are not your parents' way of doing charity—their new efforts are outside the box, adventurous, and filled with passion. It's all about people like you using their can-do attitude and resourcefulness to make good things happen.

5

Creating partnerships with nonprofits

Businesses have a long tradition of contributing to the health and vitality of the community by supporting local nonprofit organizations, such as human service agencies, environmental groups, schools, and youth organizations. For some business leaders the motivation to give is rooted in a genuine interest in supporting the community. For others, contributions are a public relations tool undertaken out of pure self-interest. We suggest that you can embrace both motivations.

You might ask, "Who cares what the motivation is?" We believe that motives do matter; they reflect your company's values, which last through changes in personnel and programs. The key is finding a contribution strategy that communicates the values you are trying to promote. What is your message to your employees if giving is based solely on the amount of media attention you receive? How likely are your customers to remember your community involvement if you are supporting causes completely unrelated to your business? We hope this chapter will inspire you to design a community program that allows you both to give from the heart *and* to maximize the impact of your contributions.

Of the three sectors of our society—public, private, and nonprofit—the nonprofit sector is arguably changing the most. This change is in response to mounting community needs as well as major funding challenges resulting from

- Tightened local and federal government budgets
- Availability of less money from foundations because of lower returns from their investment portfolios
- A proliferation of nonprofits (all vying for shrinking resources) trying to fill the void left by reductions in government social service programs
- Increased expectations of effectiveness and accountability from funders

These challenges mean nonprofits are being asked to do more with less. In response, traditional nonprofits are working to be more businesslike in their management and more innovative in raising revenue. This has led to the emergence of "enterprising nonprofits." Recently hundreds of social entrepreneurs have begun operating nonprofits that resemble for-profit enterprises. These nonprofits sell products to increase revenue, market and promote themselves like businesses, and are managed much like for-profit businesses.

This transformation of traditional nonprofits and the birthing of new enterprising nonprofits is evidence of a major change in the nonprofit world. Simultaneously, values-driven businesses are emerging that want to do more for the community and do it better.

The convergence of these two forces—enterprising nonprofits and values-driven entrepreneurs—opens up exciting opportunities for collaboration. Innovative business-nonprofit partnerships are making a substantial difference in the quality of community life. They are multiplying in numbers and expanding in scope. These partnerships are not based on the old model of dependency but on collaboration, where the community, the nonprofit, and the company all are engaged and all benefit.

How do you go about partnering with nonprofits, and how do you develop a strategy for giving? The first step is to answer questions such as these:

- What are the most pressing needs in your community?
- What unique qualities of your business can be leveraged to help you meet the community's needs?
- What activities and programs will encourage staff participation and team building and reflect company values?
- What giving strategy will have the most impact on customer loyalty, goodwill in the community, and increased sales?

The second step is to consider structural options. Successful business-nonprofit partnerships can take many forms, and most include one or more of the following:

- *Making financial contributions to a nonprofit.* The most common form of business-nonprofit partnership involves a business (or a related corporate foundation) making financial gifts to a nonprofit.
- *Making in-kind contributions.* Engaging a company's staff, vendors, and customers in providing ongoing assistance to a nonprofit in the form of noncash resources can have a profound effect on both organizations. For example, nonprofits might benefit from product donations, the use of a company's conference room, consulting time from a company's marketing staff, or the donation of used equipment.
- *Adopting a nonprofit.* Focusing financial and in-kind contributions on a specific nonprofit over a long period of time can have a transformational impact on your corporate culture and the nonprofit.

- *Creating a nonprofit.* Building a new nonprofit helps ensure a company remains engaged over the long run. Founding, guiding, and taking ownership of a compelling mission is highly energizing for the company's staff and other stakeholders and results in a strong and mutually beneficial relationship.

- *Starting a for-profit business that's owned by a nonprofit.* When a business is owned by a nonprofit organization, all of the business's practices, strategies, and profits serve the nonprofit mission rather than profit-driven shareholders.

- *Implementing cause-related marketing.* Using your product or service to promote a specific cause or nonprofit is known as cause-related marketing, or as Tom Chappell of Tom's of Maine refers to it, common good partnerships. While some companies selfishly use the name of a respected nonprofit to upgrade their own images (a tactic known as greenwashing), cause-related marketing can communicate an important message to thousands or even millions of people. Achieving similar exposure via purchasing advertisements would be well beyond the means of most nonprofits.

The final step in developing your giving strategy involves studying examples of other businesses that have done this successfully. Never miss an opportunity to learn from others! The following pages share the Hanna Andersson story and chronicle other inspiring accounts of business-nonprofit partnerships. Each one illustrates ways a business can work to benefit not only the company but the community.

Partnering with Nonprofits:
Hanna Andersson, Portland, Oregon

Hanna Andersson is a $95 million retail clothing business known for its high-quality products, family-friendly employee policies, and innovative contributions to the community through nonprofit and school partnerships. Hanna's deep community involvement was not a part of its original road map. Rather, it evolved from the principle—a commitment to quality—on which Tom and Gun Denhart founded the company in 1983. In their quest to offer high-quality children's clothing, the Denharts listened to customers, staff, and other stakeholders. This feedback was crucial to the evolution of their business.

From the outset, the Denharts wanted to create a productive, positive, and healthy working environment where employees did not have to leave their values at the door. While Hanna could pay only minimum wage in the early years, it advertised jobs that offered "more than a paycheck." As a result of genuinely listening to employees, the Denharts initiated many family-friendly programs and benefits, including

- Payment of a significant portion of their employees' child-care costs
- Flextime scheduling so staff members could create schedules that fit a variety of personal lifestyle needs
- Public transportation subsidies
- In-house yoga classes
- Paid time for volunteering in the community

At the time, these practices were quite unusual and they helped Hanna recruit and retain loyal employees. A great example of how these exceptional benefits were developed is the policy of subsidizing child care. Gun's original idea was to start a child-care center in the office. When speaking with employees, however, she found some wanted day care close to home, while others had children who were happy at their current day-care centers. Gun responded by designing a flexible program that allowed employees to more easily afford day-care programs that fit their needs. This program gave employees more peace of mind, enabled them to focus on their work, and most importantly, gave their children a good start in life.

In Hanna's second merchandise catalog, the Denharts introduced a marketing strategy that eventually became the cornerstone of the company's community involvement—Hannadowns (a play on hand-me-downs). The idea was to show that the clothing was so well made it would last beyond one child. Through the Hannadowns Clothing Donation Program, customers could send used clothing to Hanna and receive a 20 percent credit toward their next purchase. Hanna donated these clothes to nonprofits that served children in need.

The program became extraordinarily popular and took on a life of its own. In fact, it became a major driver of Hanna's growth. As the company grew, so did Hannadowns. Over the fifteen years of the program, Hanna employees sorted through stacks of donation requests from nonprofits and donated more than one million pieces of clothing to dozens of organizations. Recycling Hanna clothing eliminated waste, helped children in need, increased employee fulfillment, and fostered customer loyalty.

Having witnessed how Hannadowns helped Hanna's national reputation and sales while assisting those in need, in 1992 the company began a program to share its financial and human resources that became known as Hannashare. Gun invited an intern from an MBA program focused on socially responsible summer jobs to develop a framework for the charitable giving. The framework included two components. First, Hanna joined a growing movement of socially responsible companies committed to donating 5 percent of pretax profits to nonprofit organizations. Hanna focused its giving on children and families in need. While some years Hanna made very little or even no money, it continued to provide whatever funds, clothing, and employee time it could offer.

The second component was encouraging employee financial and in-kind donations to nonprofits. Hanna instituted two employee benefits. The Volunteer benefit paid for up to sixteen hours of volunteer hours per year, and the Employee Match benefit donated up to $500 annually per employee for his or her donations to any nonprofit of the employee's choosing. This giving framework was used for over a decade as Hanna became known for its commitment to the community and to local nonprofits through Hannashare and Hannadowns.

Eventually, the Hannadowns program grew too large to sustain. As you'll read below, Hanna made the agonizing decision to discontinue Hannadowns. Yet the program left its imprint on Hanna's mission, and the principle of pursuing the double bottom line—making a profit *and* giving back to the community—continued and flourished in new ways.

Apply Business Smarts to Your Giving

In 2001 Hanna formalized the Hannashare program by creating the Hanna Andersson Children's Foundation. With no experience in the formal grant-making process, however, the foundation made some mistakes along the way, the biggest of which was cramming too many nonprofit groups into the allocation process.

From the outset, the foundation aimed to involve employees deeply in its work. In an effort to appeal to as many employees as possible, the foundation funded a wide variety of children's groups—everything from early childhood learning, child care, and early intervention for children with disabilities to after-school programs, teen programs, and support for children affected by homelessness, substance abuse, child abuse, mental health issues, and AIDS and other medical conditions.

At a two-hour allocation meeting, employees were able to make a case for their favorite nonprofits. However, far too many presentations were made and too much information was given for people to process. The large number of nonprofit organizations created another problem. With so many groups to visit in the first few grant cycles, the program did not have enough employees to ensure every organization received a fair review.

To rectify this problem, the foundation narrowed its focus to supporting children from birth to age ten. It also gradually reduced the number of major grants awarded from twenty-one to ten. Now that the number of nonprofits has been decreased, the foundation is usually able to send two or three people on each site visit to ensure it receives balanced feedback.

Through the Hannashare program and the Hanna Andersson Children's Foundation, the company is supporting local nonprofits in communities where it does business. Hanna's employees are integrally involved in shaping the foundation's giving priorities, which fosters pride in a company that gives its employees an opportunity to *engage in* and *help* the community.

Balancing Profitability with a Costly Social Mission Program

In the mid-1990s, Hanna had grown into a $50 million business and Hanna was fast becoming an icon in the socially responsible business movement. Gun was featured on the cover of *Inc.* magazine, and Hanna was touted in other publications as a business model for the future. The Denharts never dreamed their little catalog business would grow to this size, and they certainly wouldn't have projected the dramatic increase in the amount of used clothing donated by customers nor what its costs might become.

Managing Hannadowns wasn't initially complicated because the volume was relatively small and everyone could pitch in when needed. However, while the used clothes clearly benefited vulnerable children, time was required to receive, account for, and deliver them to children's charities. The burgeoning management costs associated with these tasks were on top of the 20 percent return credits given to customers. The program that was the source of many customers' strong ties to Hanna was rapidly moving from a major company asset to a mounting liability.

In 1995 Hanna conducted market research to explore the possiblity of lowering the return credit percentage to keep the program viable. The study revealed that 95 percent of customers were familiar with Hannadowns, and 18 percent said they would change their opinion of Hanna if the credit was lowered. Hanna accepted the study's recommendation to maintain the current program.

However, that year the company lost money for the first time. This forced Hanna to cut 10 percent of its staff positions, but the company decided to leave the program intact.

By 1997 Hanna was still only marginally profitable, and the total Hannadowns credit had increased to $700,000. The handwriting was on the wall. The high costs of this in-kind program were putting the survival of the company at risk.

Gun knew that any change to the program had to be handled with great care. In early 1998 Hanna created a working group with employees from all parts of the company to explore options. They took a hard look at the program and considered what dismantling it might feel like. Digging into the numbers, they realized that only 4 percent of customers used the credit, and they asked themselves why all the other customers should subsidize a small percentage of customers.

Gun began thinking that encouraging customers to donate their clothes directly to nonprofits might be an option. Not only would it be more efficient, but it would conserve energy by reducing transportation and connect customers to local nonprofit organizations. The company would save money by discontinuing the credit and avoiding processing expenses, which would result in higher profits and more money available for grants to non-profits.

These arguments were all completely logical, but emotionally the decision was gut-wrenching. Furthermore, the group knew the company risked a public relations disaster. Hanna had become famous for—and in some ways defined by—Hannadowns. Customers loved the program, which had generated a lot of publicity through the media and awards. When Hanna failed to mention Hannadowns in just one catalog in 1992, sales plummeted—fueling speculation that customers responded less positively to Hanna without the program.

With heavy hearts, the working group in the end decided to discontinue the credit as of January 1999. Gun spent hours talking to employees, customers, and nonprofits about the reason for the change. The working group composed a letter describing the closure, suggesting that customers could donate their used Hanna clothing to charities in their community, and highlighting Hanna's policy of donating 5 percent of profits to children in need. Finally, they wrote a list of anticipated reactions from customers and the press and trained call center representatives on how to respond.

So what happened? Although Gun had worried that this closure would damage Hanna's good name, the actual negative customer response was minimal. And even more surprising to her, the year ended with a 17 percent growth in sales and a substantial increase in profitability.

The nonprofits that had received Hannadowns were of course very disappointed. However, Hanna continued to donate excess clothing to some of them. A few years later, the company began building partnerships that allowed it to remain closely connected with the nonprofit community serving children in need and created a foundation bearing the company's name.

Best Practices in Partnering with Nonprofits

While Hanna Andersson has chosen to support a number of local nonprofits through varied types of contributions, another strategy for community involvement is for a company to build a partnership with one organization that is closely aligned with the company's mission.

Adopting a Nonprofit: Wild Planet Toys, San Francisco, California

Danny Grossman cofounded his San Francisco–based company, Wild Planet Toys, with a mission to spark the imaginations of children. The company has won dozens of awards, not only for its toys but also for its community service. This success is rooted in Wild Planet's commitment to finding innovative ways to connect its employees with the community and to integrate the community, namely children, into its product development, giving the company a competitive advantage.

From the beginning, Danny was committed to giving back to the community. His early efforts included holding "play-groups" at nearby nonprofits where he would talk with children about inventing toys. During one such visit to Mercy Charities, a boy drew a picture of a device for mounting flashlights on someone's fingers. Wild Planet's design team loved the idea; the device is now known as Wild Planet's Spy Light Hand. The nine-year-old boy was the inspiration for Wild Planet's annual Kids Inventor Challenge, which asks children to submit toy ideas; the best inventions are produced and marketed, with royalties going to the young inventors.

The successful visit at Mercy Charities led Wild Planet to think about developing ongoing relationships with community organizations. If a child could draw a creation like the Spy Light Hand after one conversation, imagine what might grow out of regular visits. Danny and his staff selected an after-school program near their office and began visiting for monthly projects. They all enjoyed the activities, but Danny began to question their strategy—or lack of one. How were these visits impacting the children? How did the relationship with the nonprofit align with Wild Planet's philanthropic giving program? Was the nonprofit committed to a long-term partnership? How could he leverage this to be a competitive advantage?

Danny and his chief operating officer, Jennifer Chapman, decided to develop a more strategic approach to community involvement. Wild Planet wanted to connect with its target audience—eight- to eleven-year-old children—while dovetailing this effort with its philanthropic giving, which focused on at-risk children. Furthermore, it made sense to tie in the already successful Kids Inventor Challenge. Danny and Jennifer had also learned the importance of finding an agency where the staff members were committed to the partnership and to Wild Planet's mission.

After extensive outreach efforts, they found the Beacon Centers, a highly reputable network of after-school programs, which seemed to be a perfect fit for Wild Planet's new strategy. The Beacon Centers served the right population, and the director was prepared to provide the staff resources necessary to make a partnership work. Hesitant to make a long-term commitment too early, Wild Planet began with a one-year pilot program. The Inventor Invasion was set up as a ten-session after-school program in which Wild Planet employees volunteered to work with children through the invention process from brainstorming to prototyping. Beacon Centers' staff managed the program.

The Inventor Invasion was extremely successful. Wild Planet employees enjoyed their volunteering and felt they gained valuable knowledge from the children that they could use back in the office. Beacon Centers' staff felt the program had positive results for the children and committed to a second year. The children loved the program and demonstrated the enhanced creativity that Wild Planet had hoped for. Wild Planet agreed to continue with the partnership and contribute the funds needed to support the program. The Inventor Invasion is now entering its third year, and Wild Planet hopes to expand it to more centers in the near future.

By focusing its charitable resources on a single strategic partnership, Wild Planet was able to develop a top-notch program that benefited the company and the community. For those companies that aim to invest substantial resources and want to make a more profound difference, however, a common approach is to create a new nonprofit.

Creating Horizons for Homeless Children: Bright Horizons Family Solutions, Boston, Massachusetts

When husband-and-wife team Roger Brown and Linda Mason founded Bright Horizons Family Solutions in Boston in 1986, employer-sponsored, on-site child care was a new concept. Although the company now boasts more than 600 child-care centers in leading corporations worldwide, it took nearly six years to gain solid footing.

While building their business, Linda and Roger noticed the face of homelessness in their community changing. No longer did the homeless fit the typical image of the derelict man begging in the streets. New Englanders were seeing single mothers with children who had no place to turn. With their growing expertise in child care and education, Linda and Roger felt uniquely positioned to address the needs of homeless families. They envisioned creating community centers that would provide child care and education for homeless children and support services for their parents. But Bright Horizons was still a struggling new business. Financing a community program of this magnitude was out of the question.

Eighteen months after starting Bright Horizons, Linda and Roger decided to implement their vision by starting a nonprofit organization. This allowed them to utilize Bright Horizons' expertise to design a program and to raise funds from outside sources so as not to put a financial strain on their new company. So without telling their investors, who they feared might be concerned about the couple's divided attention, they found a graduate student to help research child homelessness. They approached the development of the soon-to-be-dubbed Horizons for Homeless Children (HHC) much like the creation of their business: by assessing community need and competition and creating an effective service delivery model.

Linda and Roger financed the start-up of HHC by writing personal checks and asking friends and family for contributions. They hired an executive director to file the necessary paperwork and begin executing the business plan. Once the organization gained official nonprofit status, they began raising charitable donations through foundations and individuals. Though Bright Horizons did not have cash to spare, the company provided valuable in-kind services, such as materials, training, office space, and employee expertise. In fact, employees were eager to be involved in the planning stages of such a worthwhile program. By 1990, HHC was ready to begin formal operations, and it was time to let Bright Horizons' investors know about the program.

To Roger and Linda's surprise, Bright Horizons' major investors were excited. Most of the investors were young venture capitalists just starting their own families, and they bought into Roger and Linda's vision for helping homeless children just as they had bought into their for-profit business plan in 1986. A majority of the investors actually joined HHC's board of directors and helped with fund-raising.

HHC has had great success. It reaches over 1,100 children weekly, has trained more than 5,000 volunteers, and provides training to other agencies at national conferences. Bright Horizons still contributes financial and in-kind assistance, but it is just one of over 1,300 donors annually who support the organization's $4 million budget and $5 million endowment.

Twenty years later, Bright Horizons has become the world's leading provider of employer-sponsored child care, early education, and work-life solutions. It has made *Fortune* magazine's list of 100 Best Companies to Work for in America for the last seven years and is on *Business Ethics* magazine's list of Best Corporate Citizens. Although their mission was purely philanthropic, Linda and Roger say the creation of HHC played a role in their company's success. It helped attract and retain employees who wanted to be involved with a company that was passionate about children and children's issues.

Common sense makes it hard to endorse the timing of their initial decision to start the foundation, but the couple maintains that companies driven by passion don't always follow a rational path. By approaching their charity work through a nonprofit, they had the freedom to let their vision take on a life of its own and grow beyond any of Bright Horizons' financial constraints. In retrospect, their charity work strengthened not only their business but also their relationships with venture capitalists, who appreciated the opportunity to make a community investment.

Bright Horizons used its business know-how to provide direct services to the community by creating a nonprofit with a similar mission. Although the company was in the business of child care and the new nonprofit had the same focus and a similar business model, Bright Horizons received no direct benefit to its financial bottom line. Tom's of Maine found a way to both leverage its core business to progress toward its social mission and connect that mission to the marketing of its products.

Cause-Related Marketing: Tom's of Maine, Kennebunk, Maine

When Tom and Kate Chappell cofounded Tom's of Maine in 1970, their vision was like that of many values-driven entrepreneurs. They wanted to develop socially responsible products, be profitable, and give back to the community. Their wide range of natural personal care products, biodegradable and recyclable packaging, and responsible product development and testing have made them a favorite among environmentally conscious customers. Annual sales of $50 million prove they can compete in the personal care industry.

Early on, the company committed 10 percent of its annual pretax profits to grants to nonprofit organizations and encouraged all employees to use 5 percent of their paid work time to volunteer for nonprofits. Although this commitment is remarkable, Tom and Kate felt it wasn't enough. They wanted to raise awareness in the community and encourage others to get involved.

Tom's designed the Common Good Partnerships (CGPs), which allowed Tom's of Maine to partner with consumers and retailers to support community projects. CGPs have three objectives: to build sales, to build awareness of a cause or social issue, and to encourage consumers and retailers to take action. The process begins with the identification of a cause and the formation of a national partnership between Tom's and a retailer. Tom's then offers awareness-building materials and point-of-sale displays and asks the retailer to use these to promote the campaign. To bring the CGP to a local level, Tom's identifies nonprofit organizations that are working on the issue in the various neighborhoods where the retailer operates.

For example, when the Longs Drugs chain became a retail partner, Tom's introduced Longs to the nonprofit Native American Health Centers in Oakland and San Francisco. To participate in the CGP, Longs committed to highlighting the centers in its Bay Area circulars and matching Tom's contribution of 2,000 tubes of toothpaste with 2,000 toothbrushes. The health centers were added to Tom's growing database of local dental clinics in need of community support. Now consumers at Bay Area Longs stores receive a free DVD and educational journal on oral health when purchasing Tom's of Maine toothpaste, and they also see a display encouraging them to get involved with the local clinics by volunteering or contributing funds through the Tom's of Maine Web site.[9]

Not only have the various local nonprofits received tangible support, but the CGPs have improved sales. During CGP promotional periods, stores report that sales of Tom's featured product are boosted by as much as 30 percent, 15 to 20 percent more than with other promotions of similar products. Redemption of CGP-related coupons, which promise $1 of every purchase will be set aside for donations to CGP nonprofits, averages 13 percent, much higher than the 3 percent national average for coupon redemption.[10]

By refusing to be content with its own grants to the nonprofit community and challenging itself to find a way to increase the number of retailers and consumers engaged in local organizations, Tom's found a profitable way to enhance everyone's contributions.

Lessons Learned: Partnering with Nonprofits

Whether your goal is to reach out to millions through a cause-related marketing campaign, to help thousands through contributions to nonprofits in your community, or to make a direct impact in the lives of the clients of a specific organization, we hope that these examples have given you a place to start. We suggest you talk with entrepreneurs and nonprofit leaders in your community to find other creative models to learn from as you build a strategy where the community, the nonprofit, and the company all benefit. As you do, keep the following lessons in mind:

- **Run the program like your business.** Designing an effective community involvement program requires patience, clearly defined goals, and often a test run. As is the case for a business profit center, specific giving strategies need to be evaluated periodically.
- **Engage employees in the process.** Including employees (who generally represent a large and diverse group) in your company's charitable giving process enables the company to make better funding decisions and keeps employees engaged in and aware of your company's efforts. Ease of entry is key when it comes to involving employees. Make the sign-up process simple and keep your requests for employees' time reasonable.
- **Connect your giving program to your core business.** Whenever possible, tie nonprofit collaborations to your company's objectives and core product or leverage the strengths of your company by developing a related product. Your company's know-how, in-kind contributions, and connections will be invaluable to the nonprofit organization, and the collaboration may provide insights that end up increasing profits.
- **Build a new nonprofit connected to your company's social mission.** Building a separate and independent nonprofit organization can advance a company's social mission far beyond what typical business-nonprofit partnerships can

accomplish. An independent nonprofit can also solicit contributions from other sources and generally will have board members who are independent from the company.

You have seen how you can build a community giving program by partnering with nonprofits—a program that will both grow local value and be good for your business. In the next chapter you will learn how businesses are fostering partnerships with the natural environment that help preserve and protect local communities.

6

Making sustainability your competitive advantage

Like most business leaders today, you are concerned about the environment and you want your business to be environmentally friendly. But what many entrepreneurs want and how they do business may be two different things. You might lack specific knowledge, or maybe business is just too crazy, so recycling and conserving energy don't quite move up to the top priority. Most of us are guilty of not paying enough attention to how our business impacts the environment. This chapter will demonstrate the awesome potential of local businesses to be successful *and* help save our planet.

Over thirty-five years after the first Earth Day and the enactment of significant government environmental regulations, and despite efforts by environmental activists of all stripes, the footprint of business on our natural world remains massive. The issue of climate change resulting from doing business on this planet is no longer a debate. The critical question now is, how much time do we have before it's too late to reverse the disastrous trends?

Paul Hawken, in his seminal book, *The Ecology of Commerce,* describes in detail how the process of commerce as it is currently practiced is using up our planet's nonrenewable resources and destroying our environment at an alarming rate.[11] In his follow-up book with Amory and Hunter Lovins, *Natural Capitalism,* he outlines the vast potential of the institution of business to end this negative spiral and begin to revitalize our ecosystem: "It is about the possibilities that will arise from the birth of a new type of industrialism, one that differs in its philosophy, goals, and fundamental processes from the industrial system that is in the standard today. These necessary changes done properly can promote economic efficiency, ecological conservation, and social equity." He goes on to describe how businesses can and must change with the times and says that those who are able to adapt not only will save our environment but will reap great financial benefits.[12]

Recognizing that the environment is a stakeholder in a business is a first step. Today entrepreneurs are going a step further and making the environment a partner in their businesses by actively seeking ways to preserve our precious planet. The environment provides a wide range of types of "natural capital"—whether energy, metal ore, or water—and is a key partner for a business. And partnering with the environment is not just a good thing to do; it's becoming the new competitive advantage. Leading entrepreneurs are embracing sustainable strategies for partnering with the environment that are either generating millions in revenues or saving them millions of dollars in expenses. Many traditional business thinkers and writers are now convinced that doing business sustainably is one of the top ways a business can increase profitability and ensure financial sustainability over the next twenty years. Environmental sustainability and financial sustainability have now become lifelong partners.

Entrepreneurs can develop sustainable partnerships with the environment by

- Creating products that are eco-friendly and help build a new culture of environmental sustainability
- Building a business that at its foundation is regenerative and mimics the functions and systems of nature
- Examining the impact that manufacturing, marketing, packaging, distributing, and disposing of a product has on the environment and making climate-friendly changes accordingly
- Joining business organizations committed to building an environmentally sustainable community and searching for ways to influence other local businesses and their stakeholders to operate environmentally responsibly
- Collaborating with nonprofit and governmental organizations to promote eco-friendly business practices and support community-based environmental projects

This chapter features inspirational stories of environmentally conscious entrepreneurs who have found ways to develop tangible partnerships with the environment in order to minimize their negative impact and maximize their positive effect on our fragile ecosystem—and they've done this while improving the bottom line. They show us how partnering with the environment is a major competitive advantage that can serve as a foundation for future business growth.

For Will Raap and Gardener's Supply, doing business in harmony with the environment is second nature. Will's business sets the standard for partnering with the environment, and it is nearly impossible to draw a line between what it does to improve our ecosystem and the sources of its profitability.

Partnering with the Environment: Gardener's Supply, Burlington, Vermont

The mission of Gardener's Supply is to "Improve the world through gardening." Gardner's Supply is a national catalog and

Internet company (with two retail stores in Vermont) that helps people have more fun and success in their organic gardens by offering everything from organic fertilizer and garden furniture to flower supports and greenhouses.

The products of Gardener's Supply clearly contribute to the health of customers and the environment. But what really distinguishes this company from other green businesses is its relationship with its neighborhood. From the very beginning, Gardener's Supply has proactively worked to improve the local community, and this work has grown into a dynamic partnership with the local environment.

In 1985 Gardener's Supply had outgrown its original location and needed to move to a larger site. Its founder, Will Raap, decided to move to the site of an abandoned pig slaughterhouse in an area near Burlington, Vermont, known as the Intervale (because it is low-lying land next to the Winooski River).

As Will told us, "By most measures, it was a stupid place to go. It was literally a dump located on the wrong side of the tracks. The commerce of drug deals and stolen cars long ago had replaced a rich agricultural heritage. But for us, it seemed just perfect. It was close to downtown Burlington and in a low-income area, it had acres of unused land, and it was adjacent to an innovative wood-burning power plant. Ultimately, it was a place where we could be a catalyst to make good things happen."

And making good things happen in this rundown part of Burlington was exactly what the company did and continues to do. The Intervale is a haven for diverse wildlife, and it's a fertile floodplain with hundreds of acres of tillable land. Its agricultural heritage goes back to the Abenaki indigenous peoples who first farmed there thousands of years ago.

Vermont's founding father, Ethan Allen, and other colonial settlers arrived in the eighteenth century, and for over 200 years the Intervale produced flax, dairy products, pork, barley, lumber, and potash. Sadly, by 1960 it had degenerated into an informal junkyard, then a city landfill, and finally a haven for crime. This was the state of affairs at the Intervale when Will Raap and company moved in.

From the beginning, Will's stated purpose was to restore the Intervale's agricultural heritage and its original natural beauty. Setting up shop in this undesirable area had an immediate positive impact because it brought a vibrant and environmentally responsible business to the neighborhood.

One of the company's first initiatives was starting a community composting program that has become a national model. Another major step was taken in 1990, when Will, Gardener's Supply, and others formed the Intervale Foundation (now called the Intervale Center). Its mission is to develop land and farm-based enterprises to generate economic and social opportunity while protecting natural resources. Although Will was the visionary behind the formation of the Intervale Center, and Gardener's Supply remains very active in the center's programs, it is an independent nonprofit organization with a separate board.

Since 1985 the Intervale Center has reclaimed over 325 acres for agricultural use, and its long-range plan calls for owning or leasing most of this land within five years. Today thirteen organic farms produce 600,000 pounds of healthy food for the community and contribute over $1 million to the local economy. The Intervale Farms Program provides land and equipment as well as business and marketing services for these thriving organic farms.

The Intervale Center encourages self-supporting enterprises that utilize and protect the unique natural assets of the Intervale while financially contributing to its revitalization. These land-based ventures are part of an overall strategy of embedding economic systems locally by capitalizing on emerging free market opportunities. As a result, this blossoming ecosystem hosts twenty-one restoration enterprises, including farms and other enterprises. The Intervale has essentially become a green industrial park offering an incubator for environmentally and economically sound business and farming models.

A terrific example of the center's strategy is the Intervale Compost Program started by Gardener's Supply and now folded into the Intervale Center. When negotiating the move of Gardener's Supply to the Intervale, Will looked for every opportunity to leverage this relocation for the benefit of the community. He was able to persuade Burlington mayor Bernie Sanders (now a U.S. congressman) to offer city support for the creation of a compost center for leaves and yard waste. This led to the 1988 founding of the Intervale's first venture—Intervale Compost Products.

A community composting program provides multiple benefits to the environment. First, it saves landfill space because over one-quarter of all material that ends up in landfills could have been composted. Second, the resulting organic compost helps restore and revitalize the depleted soils of farms and gardens.

Gardener's Supply began this innovative program by sending notices in residents' utility bills asking them to bring their leaves to the new composting center in the Intervale. Not only was there no charge to the residents, but as an additional incentive, those who brought in leaves in the fall could pick up two bushels of compost the following spring. Much to the surprise of Will and his team, thousands of residents took them up on this offer.

Now the challenge was to follow through on their bold promise. Composting tons of leaves was a relatively new process, and Gardener's Supply found itself on a steep learning curve. Creating quality compost is an art much like cooking: you need the right ingredients added at just the right times.

This is where being an entrepreneurial company came in handy. Gardener's Supply's leadership was agile enough to make adjustments to the process and to marshal the necessary resources to make it work. As an example, 20 percent of the compost ingredients needed to be nitrogen, so the leaders tracked down manure from local farmers. They trucked in waste water from the Ben & Jerry's Ice Cream production process because compost needs moisture and the milk protein improved the compost recipe, plus it was a much better way for Ben & Jerry's to dispose of this waste stream. They brought in a farm tractor to continually turn the massive amount of leaves, they acquired an old Little League backstop through which to screen the leaves, and they appropriated an old lawn mower engine to shake the screen to produce uniform compost.

Intervale Compost Products has grown to become Vermont's leading compost operation, recycling 20,000 tons of leaves, sawdust, cow manure, food scraps, and ice cream waste each year and converting it into more than 10,000 tons of finished compost. The compost is used for a wide range of agricultural and horticultural products. For the past nine years, this venture has had a substantial cash surplus, which helps cover the Intervale Center's annual operating expenses.

The composting program has also played a key role in the revitalization of the Intervale because it has helped rebuild the soil after years of abuse. To begin with, the soil contained $1/2$ percent organic matter. To be economically viable organic farm land, the soil needed 3 to 5 percent organic matter. Finished compost was spread on farmland in the Intervale, helping to restore the soil and bring healthy, organic produce to local residents.

And on top of all this good produced by the compost, the program now receives tipping fees paid by companies dropping off organic waste. These fees have increased to the point where the program has become a profit center for the Intervale Center, which helps finance other new projects.

But as groundbreaking as the Intervale Center is, it isn't the only way that Gardener's Supply contributes to the local natural environment. Five years ago, the company began the Practice Random Acts of Gardening program, which encourages people of all ages to garden. Staff members build and deliver in-ground or container-based gardens to community squares, nonprofits, and local businesses. This program has helped local residents start hundreds of gardens in the Burlington area.

It's Not Good Business If It Doesn't Make Money

As you have seen, Gardener's Supply is an imaginative outfit. And as you might guess, some of the company's efforts to combine its values with making money may have made sense in theory but didn't work in reality. In the hard, cold reality of business, fresh ideas that look like hot business opportunities may turn to ice when rolled out in the marketplace. One Gardener's Supply idea for promoting environmental uses of water did turn to ice and cost the company thousands of dollars. Will and his team have learned the hard way and they're now the wiser for it.

Will and his management team are always on the lookout for a new product or idea that will make a difference in the world and make the company money. Sometimes their enthusiasm for changing the world has blurred their vision to the economic viability of a new project.

Fifteen years ago Gardener's Supply introduced a distinct new Water Wise catalog because Will and his team believed water was a scarce and valuable resource, like oil, that needed to be conserved, managed, and reused when possible. The catalog offered water collection devices such as cisterns and rain barrels, water purification systems, gray water usage options, and the like. Unfortunately, this catalog was way ahead of its time and the products didn't sell. Two years later the losing venture was shut down, costing the company over $100,000 and untold hours of management time.

The Gardener's Supply culture rewards entrepreneurial effort, in particular those efforts aimed at changing the world. Losing efforts like Water Wise have made an impression on Gardener's Supply, and the management team is more seasoned and more cautious. Each new product or venture is now carefully researched to make sure it has a reasonable chance to succeed and is worth the financial risk.

Gardener's Supply remains committed to experimentation and to taking calculated risks because business innovation can happen only when a company is willing to make a few mistakes. Will and his team aim to decrease the number of serious mistakes, and they work to ensure the potential downside is less disastrous. On the flip side, no amount of research can predict the success of a new product. The only real test is to bring it to market. A company committed to long-term success must strike a balance between a passionate belief in a new product and hard core business analysis.

Balancing the Need for Marketing Materials with a Concern for Increasing the Waste Stream

Balancing your values with the practical reality of doing business is a constant challenge. Gardener's Supply is a catalog company that sends out attractive catalogs promoting environmentally friendly products that some recipients consider nothing but junk mail. This presents a real contradiction that the management is addressing every day.

Figuring out how to market a product successfully and at the same time wanting to reduce your impact on the environment is a conundrum that environmentally conscious entrepreneurs have struggled with for years and now demands even more attention. This is particularly vexing for a catalog company because direct-mail marketing is a cost-effective way to reach new customers. Unfortunately, when a company rents lists of potential customers and sends its catalogs, orders will result from only a small percentage (usually 2 to 3 percent depending on the product and the list). This means that 97 to 98 percent of the catalogs are discarded as junk mail, and most of them end up in landfills. Not only is this expensive for the company, but it wastes paper and energy in printing and mailing and is a major contributor to the nation's solid waste stream. What's a values-based entrepreneur to do?

Gardener's Supply has taken a variety of steps to deal with this management tension. Its first step in the 1980s was to establish a community recycling program for Chittenden County. The collection site accepted glossy paper used in catalogs (most recycling programs wouldn't accept glossy paper in those days). The paper was then trucked to a company in New Jersey that would recycle it. This program was such a success that a year later the Chittenden Solid Waste District took over the administration of this program. Will commented, "Now we are responsible for recycling more glossy paper than we mail out, so we have in effect developed the solid waste version of a 'carbon credit exchange.' We also convinced our main printer, Quad/Graphics, to do the same in communities where their plants are across the country. On top of this we keep the cycle moving by using 35 percent or higher of postconsumer recycled paper for our catalogs."

As a direct result of Gardener's Supply's work, the local government body broadened its recycling programs for the whole community and the program has become a revenue source for the county.

Encouraging customer use of the Internet has been another potential answer to this business paradox. Nearly 50 percent of all Gardener's Supply orders are now being made over the Internet. However, even though the company has made a major investment in technology and built an attractive Web site, it has not yet found a way to eliminate the catalogs. People still like the look and feel of traditional catalogs they can read at their leisure, and they use the catalogs to guide their online orders. But thanks to its Web site, Gardener's Supply has been able to print fewer catalogs while generating more sales. It has also decreased the paper and transportation costs incurred by mailing out confirmations, change orders, and other communications that are nearly all handled via e-mail now.

Gardener's Supply has also made managing mailing lists a science. For example, "data cleanliness" is important, and the company takes great care to ensure old addresses are kept out, households that may be on more than one list receive only one catalog, and no one receives a catalog who doesn't want one. In general, people who haven't made a purchase for three catalogs are taken off the list.

Like most management tensions, this business riddle has no easy answers. Will Raap's answer is to make the resolution of this environmental challenge an ongoing business priority.

Best Practices in Partnering with the Environment

The Gardener's Supply model can help you create your own vision for how your business can partner with the environment to grow local value. The next example shows how Guy Bazzani melds his construction company's commitment to strengthening an inner-city community with green building practices. This merging of missions is a preview of things to come.

Revitalizing and Preserving an Inner-City Neighborhood: Bazzani Associates, Grand Rapids, Michigan

In 1981 Guy Bazzani founded his construction and development firm, Bazzani Associates. Today he is the sole owner of an architecture, construction, and real estate firm with $4 million in annual revenues.

Guy was committed to a triple bottom line—people, planet, and profits—long before this term was in vogue. Guy and Bazzani Associates use their years of experience and technical ingenuity to partner with the natural environment to help build strong and inviting communities. They effectively leverage natural resources such as sunlight, rain, and soil in a cooperative manner to create systems that ultimately cost their clients less and provide greater value.

An entrepreneur who lives his grand vision every day, Guy believes in the importance of green building and the power of positive economic and community development. He can't do one without the other. Because he's been a designer-builder and developer in Grand Rapids for twenty-five years, you can see the results of his work by walking the streets of this racially diverse urban area.

The construction of his current office is a great example of how Guy and his company do their work. When Guy purchased the historic brick buildings built in 1918, they had been abandoned and were being used by drug dealers. The neighborhood needed revitalization and had been redlined by banks as an area that was not to receive loans. Guy saw the potential for the buildings and the neighborhood. He then began to work with neighborhood residents and city officials to design a plan that was historically appropriate and supported the livability and growth of the community. In large part because of his transparency and willingness to listen and because he did what he promised, his new buildings received accolades from all racial groups in the community.

The rebuilt 30,000-square-foot group of mixed-use historic buildings covers a whole block and anchors a corner in the neighborhood and has kept its classic character and 1920s feel. It's now much more open and inviting and currently houses the offices of Bazzani Associates, Guy's personal home, and a collection of office and retail uses that have brought new economic life to this previously deteriorated neighborhood.

The structure is a state-of-the-art "green building" that was the first building in Grand Rapids to achieve a silver-level Leadership in Energy and Environmental Design (LEED) certification, a national standard for environmentally responsible building. This certification is extremely detailed in its requirements, and achieving it is no small feat.

Bazzani Associates installed dual flush toilets that use only 0.8 gallon per flush (compared to 1.6 gallons for low-flush toilets and 3 gallons for standard ones). The building was constructed with sustainable and nontoxic materials, and most of the construction waste was recycled. Although finishing products such as glues and paints have been improved in recent years, the fumes they give off remain a challenge. Bazzani used products that give off a minimum of gases, such as prefinished bamboo. Once the building was complete, fresh air was pumped in for two weeks to flush out the building. All of this work created an elegant, healthy, and functional building that could be heated for $.58 per square foot (2004) at a time when the average cost to heat a building in Grand Rapids was $2.00 per square foot.

Guy and his team soon found their next project in the neighborhood. By collaborating with neighborhood groups and local foundations, Bazzani Associates purchased a brownfield site located at a critical corner in the adjoining East Hills neighborhood. The process of remediating this site was complicated and involved removing contaminated material up to twenty-five feet deep. It ultimately cost the previous owner (an oil company) over $550,000. The result is what is known today as the East Hills Center—a five-unit retail condominium that meets the Secretary of the Interior's Standards for New Buildings in Historic Districts. Guy and his team designed a context-sensitive building that achieved a LEED gold certification. They superinsulated the building and designed it for maximum passive solar heat. Utilizing daylight-harvesting technology, they connected light sensors with automatic dimmers to maximize natural light and minimize artificial light. The building incorporates the same water conservation methods and material selection as the Bazzani Associates building.

Storm-water management is becoming a major issue in construction projects. Unless captured, the water that runs off a site flows into the streets, where it becomes contaminated with brake and tire dust. If it flows into a river, that river is toxic to all life.

The East Hills Center is a half-acre site designed to have zero storm-water discharge and is not connected to the city storm-water system. All rainwater either evaporates or recharges the groundwater. The building has a green roof that is a garden of a succulent, drought-resistant sedum that absorbs water and holds it. In the summer, the water evaporation cools the building. Storm water from the parking lot drains into a garden of plants and a biomass that filters the contaminants coming off the lot.

All of this good, green building was done in a manner sensitive to the character of this historic district. In fact, Guy went so far as to put a deed restriction on the property mandating that any architectural changes must be approved by the local neighborhood association.

For Guy Bazzani and his company, partnering with the environment to improve the community is just part of doing business—it's what they're all about. And this is also what Seven Stars Yogurt is all about. Its story features a biodynamic dairy farm that grew into a food processing business that honors the land and the animals that provide the food—a creative way to save a family dairy farm and help preserve open space and limit suburban sprawl.

Producing and Processing Nutritious Food: Seven Stars Yogurt, Phoenixville, Pennsylvania

David Griffiths calls himself a child of the seventies. He went to college at the University of California at Santa Cruz, where he realized that he was a better farmer than student. His next stop was Emerson College in England, where he studied biodynamic agriculture and the philosophy of Rudolf Steiner, an early twentieth-century Austrian philosopher, scientist, educator, and mystic. Steiner's insights guided him to form a variety of systems, including Waldorf Schools and a form of organic farming known as biodynamics.

After his stint at Emerson, David returned to California and earned a bachelor's degree in soil science. He worked at several large conventionally managed farms in California to gain additional farming experience. Eventually David had his fill of chemically based farms and called his friend Edie, whom he had met at Emerson. She invited him to join her and work at the Hawthorne Valley Farm, a Steiner community in New York. David didn't see himself as a dairy farmer, but Edie's charm persuaded him to join her at Hawthorne Valley. It wasn't long before they were married, and shortly after they moved to Kimberton Farms, owned by the Kimberton Waldorf School. The farm was producing buckets of milk and losing buckets of money. Edie and David leased the farm (renaming it Seven Stars Farm) and purchased the equipment and began producing and selling organic bottled milk at a small store located in the milk processing plant. While the store's sales of natural foods flourished, demand for bottled milk was flat.

This problem inspired them to begin a new milk processing venture—making organic yogurt. Seven Stars Organic Yogurt was introduced to the natural foods market in 1990, and before long it was a profitable venture. An important piece of this success was the connections the couple had made with natural foods wholesalers while running the retail store. This enabled them to gain widespread distribution of their yogurt in a relatively short period. The popularity of their organic yogurt, the unprofitability of the milk-bottling business, and the growth of the retail store led them to shut down the bulky milk-bottling process. By 1994, the retail store had outgrown its space and, under new ownership, moved to its current location in a Phoenixville retail district.

For the first ten years that Seven Stars grew, David and Edie improved their yogurt making and distribution systems as they went along. Then in 2000 a large round bale of hay fell on David, and the accident left him a quadriplegic. The Kimberton community came together to support David and Edie and the continuation of their business. Friends organized a community-wide effort to retrofit the farmhouse so that David could continue to live there. In the four-month period that David was in the hospital, a 1,000-square-foot addition was built using primarily volunteer labor. David no longer can do the physical tasks of dairy farming, but he still can help with the task of managing Seven Stars Farm.

Since 2000 Seven Stars has continued to experience slow, consistent growth. By 2006 the company had $1.4 million in revenues, eight full-time employees, and four to six part-time workers. David and Edie are providing high-quality organic yogurt to their community and much of the Eastern United States, while making a living dairy farming in suburbia. But they are doing much more—they are making major contributions to their community and its environment.

The Seven Stars contribution to the ecosystem begins with the term "biodynamic agriculture," a system developed in 1926 that predates organic farming by twenty years or more. Biodynamic agriculture is a system of caring for the land and raising animals or crops based on a spiritual philosophy that has proven practical benefits but is sometimes difficult to explain. Biodynamic farmers view the farm as a complete organism within which nutrients are recycled. David and Edie view their business and the environment as one and the same; they can't distinguish between the two. Doing something that would damage the environment would be unthinkable since it would simultaneously damage their business. Partnering with the environment to improve the community is integral to their spiritual values and their philosophy of doing business.

At Seven Stars the cows are respected and cared for. They are allowed to graze and are outdoors most of the day and night seven months of the year and are outdoors at least part of the day during the five cold months. David and Edie farm in a way that allows the cattle to live naturally and symbiotically with the land.

Seven Stars rotates the fields for grazing, a process that is good not only for the cows and their milk but also for the land. Keeping meadows alive with a stable grass cover all year round prevents soil erosion and contributes to the ecosystem in other ways as well.

Seven Stars also is a living laboratory for the children in the community. The farm is located directly across the street from the Kimberton Waldorf School, and every student knows Edie and David and loves visiting the cows and learning about farming.

If you visit the Phoenixville, Pennsylvania, area you'll see hillsides that were once fertile farmland covered with new subdivisions or brown scars of land that have been graded for home construction. Seven Stars has preserved its land as open space, a major victory for the environment in these times of suburban sprawl.

Despite the standard challenges of managing a farm and a business, competition from corporate agribusiness, and personal physical challenges, David and Edie built a profitable dairy farm and yogurt business that is in a spiritual and commercial partnership with the local environment and the cultural life of the Kimberton community. In this process they've kept acres of land as open space, provided well-paying jobs for community residents, offered hands-on education for hundreds of children, and produced healthy and delicious yogurt made from the milk of humanely treated cows.

Lessons Learned: Partnering with the Environment

Following are some of the lessons the entrepreneurs highlighted in this chapter have learned about partnering with the environment:

- **Grow profits by being green.** Doing business in an environmentally sustainable manner has become an important way for businesses to ensure financial sustainability. Marketing "green" products, partnering with nonprofits and government agencies, and saving money on energy bills through conservation measures or the purchase of new equipment are only some of the ways green business practices can grow profits.
- **Be green (it's contagious).** When you take a strong stand for protecting the environment by making your business a model for sustainable business practices, other stakeholders will join you. Setting high standards for your own company

raises the bar for everyone, and a positive community synergy takes hold.

- **Be in the black to stay green.** Profitability is mandatory if you want to do good work in the community. When you roll out a new mission-driven product, it is important that the financial downside doesn't put the company at risk. Be bold, but move cautiously by taking measures to make certain your desire to change the world doesn't blind you to the realities of the marketplace and the need for a positive cash flow.

- **Practice the art of compromise.** Choosing to manage a business often means learning the art of compromise, and as a values-driven entrepreneur you must learn to walk a difficult line. No business is perfect, and most companies leave a negative footprint on our environment. The objective is to keep your business profitable while minimizing the negative impact. Engage your company in a long-term quest to find environmentally friendly solutions to challenging problems.

Gardener's Supply, Bazzani Associates, and Seven Stars Yogurt all offer great examples of how your company can partner with the environment, and they have set the bar high. Most likely you haven't been thinking about how your business can partner with the government to grow local value. The following chapter offers innovative examples of how your company can build bridges to government agencies for the betterment of your community and the growth of your business.

7

Collaborating with government

Local, state, and federal governments all have much to gain from the success of your business. When your vision includes collaboration with government agencies, partnerships are possible that benefit both your business and your community.

Governmental bureaucracies, regulations, and other hurdles may have scared you away from developing successful business-government partnerships. You may think you don't have the necessary time or patience. But times are changing, and business-government collaboration has become an important concept for the twenty-first century. If building your business and growing local value is your goal, then looking for ways to work with government agencies should be on your agenda.

Your business can choose from a wide variety of methods for constructing bridges with government agencies to build a stronger community. The list below offers basic categories of government-business partnerships.

- *Public school partnerships.* As federal, state, and local budgets have tightened, funding of public schools has suffered.

This has opened up opportunities for businesses and schools to collaborate.

- *Municipal government efforts to support local independent businesses.* The dominance of chains and big-box stores has resulted in local retail stores going out of business and leaving many downtown areas deserted and boarded-up. In response, networks of locally owned businesses have organized Local First campaigns in communities all over North America. Several municipalities and local government officials have recognized the importance of independent businesses to sustainable economic development and have partnered with and helped fund these campaigns.
- *Municipal, state, and federal initiatives to create a sustainable community.* Mayors from cities and towns of all sizes are developing "sustainable" or "green" initiatives to create more sustainable communities. These include recycling programs, green building projects, inner-city development, and energy conservation. Values-based business leaders are playing a pivotal role in several of these initiatives.
- *Services for government agencies.* Many businesses have government agencies as their primary customers. Although privatization (moving government services into the private sector) has obvious limitations, governments at all levels have needs that are best met by a commercial enterprise. When the public and private sectors build bridges in order to work together, the community usually wins.
- *Business expansions.* A common source of conflict between business and government emerges when a business moves to expand its physical plant. Dealing with government officials, neighbors, and government regulations can sorely test an entrepreneur's patience. However, values-driven entrepreneurs respect the legitimate rights of the community and proactively look for solutions that meet everyone's needs.

(Abuses of public-private partnerships obviously occur when politics and lobbying play a role in determining which company wins a contract.)

The American Reading Company understands the potential of partnering with government agencies. The company's business model relies on working with local school systems and on gaining government funding for the development of its programs. Jane Hileman has created a terrific example of how a business can build bridges with government agencies and create a more culturally and economically just world.

Partnering with Government Agencies:
The American Reading Company, Philadelphia, Pennsylvania

Jane Hileman began teaching school in 1973. While working at an urban middle school in North Philadelphia, she created programs to help her students do well on standardized tests. After she had worked with them for two years, all of her students scored in the 90th percentile on the California Achievement Test (at that time the standard reading test in most states). This success wasn't at all surprising to Jane, but it did give her concrete evidence of what she intuitively knew—there is no excuse for the achievement gap that exists between students in rich communities and those in poor communities. She felt that it was imperative that educators like her figure out how to help *all* children succeed.

She knew that successful people pass on their penchant for achievement to their children through teaching the use of language and living the "lifestyle of reading." She also knew that integrating reading into a family's daily rituals makes reading as natural as breathing. Jane's mission was to give poor children access to the same literary life that wealthy children get. This meant being read to every day and eventually reading on their own every day.

By 1995 Jane's work had evolved to become a practical and simple system that she felt could change the world. Now she needed to get it into schools so it could be used. But how best to do this? At first she tried to market her reading system from her position as a teacher within the school structure. She succeeded in persuading several schools and individual teachers in Philadelphia to embrace the program, but she had to fund much of this work out of her own pocket. At that point no school systems would adopt her program. They tend to be slow to accept change, and innovation from within is rarely tolerated.

Not to be deterred, Jane began working through the nonprofit world, eventually starting her own tax-exempt nonprofit organization. This didn't work either, and she became frustrated with the ineffectiveness of her nonprofit strategy. She realized that if she was going to take her idea to market she would have to go directly to the customer. She had become an entrepreneur with a social mission, and she wanted to get moving. Filled with a sense of urgency, she joined the ranks of entrepreneurs, and in 1998 Jane started the American Reading Company (ARC).

After eight years the American Reading Company has 105 employees, with revenues of almost $15 million, and has averaged 70 percent growth since its founding. Its profits are plowed back into the company to facilitate its objective of rapid expansion. Although ARC has outside investors, Jane has maintained the controlling interest in her company, which she feels has enabled ARC to remain true to its mission, even when money got tight. As of early 2006, ARC is providing successful reading programs to 250,000 children in 29 states and 1,050 schools.

The core ARC program is the 100 Book Challenge. It is a state-of-the-art, standards-based reading program that teaches students to read, parents to create a literacy-rich home environment, and teachers how to teach reading using trade books.

Twenty thousand children's book titles are organized into plastic bins, based on reading levels, and brought into schools to form classroom libraries that circulate weekly. Brightly colored skills cards outline what readers need to be able to do to read at each level using state standards, so they know where they stand and what they need to do to improve. Students are required to read for a minimum of thirty minutes a day from books they can read and want to read. Teachers use a Readers' Workshop model to teach students not only how to read but why they should read.

ARC's Research Labs and its new product, Curriculum Integration Project, both provide libraries and curricula in social studies and science so every student can access grade-level content standards while reading at their individual success level.

Getting ARC off the ground was tough. Despite Jane's view that she was offering a stellar product that would make a big difference in the lives of children, during weeks of making pitches she received one no after another. Of course, getting turned down day after day is not a new experience for a budding entrepreneur. And, as Jane points out, this new venture gave her innumerable opportunities to test herself in what she calls the three Rs of successful entrepreneurship—resourcefulness, resilience, and relentlessness.

The years spent putting the program into Philadelphia schools on a nonprofit basis finally paid off. Shortly before Thanksgiving 1997, an article appeared in the *Philadelphia Inquirer* with the headline "Reading Program Gets Rave Reviews."[13] This inspired the ABELL Foundation (which is dedicated to enhancing the quality of life in Baltimore and Maryland) to call and invite her to Baltimore to present the program. Shortly after her presentation, the foundation cut a $140,000 check to ARC for providing a summer reading program in Baltimore. This was the beginning of a long, successful relationship that opened the doors for ARC into other cities.

For example, the Akron school system began the 100 Book Challenge as a summer school program in 1998, and the program has since spread to over twenty schools in Akron. In 2005 Akron added the ARC Research Labs to its summer school program as a companion to the 100 Book Challenge. Another great example is the Jersey City school system, which includes the 100 Book Challenge in all of its grade 1–5 schools. It has also adopted the ARC Research Labs for its middle schools as part of its language arts curriculum district-wide.

AMETEK, a $3 billion international aeronautics instrument company headquartered in Paoli, Pennsylvania, has been a big supporter of the ARC program. The 100 Book Challenge is one of the literacy programs sponsored by the AMETEK Foundation. The foundation placed the program into thirty classrooms in two schools in Binghamton, New York, in 2002 and has since instituted it in Rochester, New Jersey; Panther Valley, Pennsylvania; and West Chicago, Illinois. It not only provides the program but continues to support it in each of these locations for three to five years. The school systems in these cities continue to use the 100 Book Challenge with varying degrees of support from AMETEK, and they have decided to implement the program at their own expense when AMETEK's support is no longer available.

The more ARC becomes involved in school systems throughout the United States, the more glaring the need for effective reading programs becomes. As Jane says, "The bottom line is that children who are below grade level in reading need to move two to fours years in reading levels in one year. That's a big job—and one we're up to. We preach the idea that if you are not a reader, you can become one and here's a way for you to do it. It works, and the rewards last a lifetime."

ARC utilizes a project-based learning model, and the children become invested in the project of their own choice in which they read and write and talk and listen in a group of peers. The teachers become coaches of the students, explaining what they are expected to learn by the end of the unit and working with them to achieve the objectives. Jane has found that if you make the standards clear at the beginning and map out a pathway to success, the children learn to read.

What's remarkable about the work of ARC is that as much as the program effectively teaches children to read, it's not solely about the reading. It's as much about agency and creating a fertile environment that allows young people to flourish. Reading becomes simply the entry point for children to grow and thrive. Jane views this as an entrepreneurial model because each child creates what could be viewed as a business plan. The child sets objectives and plots a strategy, and the educators and ARC provide the support to help all the children achieve their goals. Jane has found that the skills the children acquire in learning to read today can be directly transferred to learning how to get what they want in the future.

And ARC is crystal clear that involving parents in the process is indispensable to its success and encourages their participation from the get-go. When parents understand what ARC is asking them to do, they feel more in control and more relaxed. The process of learning to read becomes a partnership and a family affair with its attendant direct and indirect benefits.

As ARC has grown, it has greatly increased the number of staff members, all of whom are highly competent and fully committed to the mission of the company. Hiring and training staff is always a challenge. As a way of attracting and keeping talented people, Jane has created an emotionally and spiritually rewarding work environment. This supportive culture enables ARC's staff to sustain the saint-like patience needed to partner with hundreds of different schools all over the country.

Partner with Those Who Have the Most at Stake

Partnering with school systems and government bureaucracies is daunting, so much so that many entrepreneurs won't even attempt it. And these fears do have their basis in fact. ARC knows how difficult a task it is to build partnerships with school systems. The company uses every possible opportunity to spread the word through media features, innumerable speaking engagements at conferences and meetings, and most important, word of mouth. As the ARC program grew and established a track record, the marketing materials shared the results and possibilities, and much less persuasion was needed.

Jane continues to present her case whenever and wherever possible. Occasionally, a school board or government leader will sign on, but she has learned the hard way that her primary strategy should be to work locally with teachers and school administrators in order to gain their buy-in. These educators see the need for ARC's program every day, and they know the ins and outs of the various bureaucracies. Once they become excited about the program, they usually find creative ways to obtain the necessary funding.

Balancing Passion with Patience

Jane and her staff are passionate about teaching children to read. They want to improve reading programs, and they want to do it now. Billions of dollars of federal funding are available for education. One would think that the process of obtaining official governmental approval for funding might take time, but eventually a program like ARC would be an approved program. This has not been the case, and it's been so frustrating for Jane and her team.

ARC prides itself in its ability to work through the morass of government regulations. Jane and her staff make painstaking efforts to get access to decision makers and other key people in positions of influence in order to make their case effectively. Jane was appointed to the National Association for Educational Progress steering committee, which tracks reading progress around the nation, and she has spoken at over 150 conferences. Several large-scale studies were done by Temple University and others, demonstrating the effectiveness of the program. Even with all the documented results and her active networking, the state of Pennsylvania has not approved the program for purchase by schools using money for Reading First, a federal reading program.

Jane's frustration with obtaining funding for her program has gone beyond Pennsylvania. President Bush's No Child Left Behind program has set aside billions of dollars to improve the education of all children, and schools across the country have been told by their states that they can purchase programs from two short lists of approved programs. In spite of an excellent reputation backed up by strong empirical data, ARC has not yet been able to get on either of these lists. For the first two years of No Child Left Behind, the American Reading Company was told it must have scientifically proven results from a randomized child study that can cost up to a million dollars. This requirement favors large corporations and effectively prevents small companies with new and innovative ideas from participating in this important federal program. Jane hopes that as the program continues to grow, even this formidable wall will come down.

Best Practices in Partnering with Government Agencies

Jane and ARC partner with school systems to improve reading skills by offering an effective and proven reading program. Powell's Books, one of the nation's outstanding independent bookstores, is also partnering with local school systems to promote reading, but it is doing this by putting books in the hands of thousands of schoolchildren.

Encouraging Children to Read More: Powell's Books, Portland, Oregon

Powell's Books opened in 1971 on a derelict corner in northwest Portland, Oregon. Powell's now has six locations throughout the city, a successful Web site, and annual revenues over $20 million. Despite the business's tremendous growth and success, what locals love about Powell's is its continued commitment to being a neighborhood bookstore, with a staff that cares deeply about books and the community.

For the last nine years, the center of Powell's community giving program has been the It's for Kids campaign. President Michael Powell began the campaign as a way to partner with local public schools to encourage young people to read and hopefully to boost holiday sales. If a customer mentioned It's for Kids at the check stand, Powell's gave a credit of 10 percent of the purchase to the public schools to be used by school librarians for book purchases. The program reinforced the company's image as community oriented and heightened public awareness of the needs of public schools. Although Powell's found that the program did not make a difference in the sales for the holiday season, Powell's continued the program, donating over 40,000 books to local public schools between 1995 and 2004.

Powell's always received a great deal of positive feedback from grateful parents, teachers, and school librarians. And over the years, as funding for Oregon schools was gradually cut, school librarians began to depend on Powell's program. Recognizing this increasing need, in 2005 Michael Powell decided it was time for a change. As implemented, the program provided librarians with credits to purchase books from Powell's at retail prices. Michael thought there must be a way to expand this partnership and to leverage his staff's book-buying expertise to significantly increase the flow of books into local schools while not increasing the expense to Powell's.

The redesigned program, School Book Challenge, would encourage customers to contribute the equivalent of one book, valued at $5.95. In turn, Powell's would match each pledge with ten additional books. The difference? Instead of giving librarians a cash credit, Powell's staff would choose the books, using their expertise to select an appropriate assortment that could be acquired more cheaply by buying in bulk and partnering with vendors interested in helping a good cause.

Librarians' initial responses to this new idea were not overwhelmingly positive. They continued to be gracious but expressed disinclination for any change to the program that was often their sole source of new books. In response, Powell's staff convened meetings with groups of librarians, listened to their concerns, and tried to reassure them that the new program would be more successful than It's for Kids had ever been. In the end, despite the schools' hesitations, Powell's went ahead with the innovative idea.

In August 2005, 275 teachers and librarians from ninety public schools were invited to the Powell's warehouse for book selection. To their surprise, they found over 57,000 books—more than had been donated in the entire history of the It's for Kids program! The librarians were overwhelmed by the selection and number of books. Through this innovative business and government partnership, schools received between 400 and 800 books each, meaning an average tenfold increase over the 60 or so books they had received in years past.

What ARC and Powell's Books are doing to support reading programs in local school systems is impressive. New Seasons Market intentionally partnered with residents and the local government to grow its business in an environmentally friendly manner. And the good news is that the collaboration was successful, offering an excellent example for how your company can build bridges to help grow local value.

Constructing an Environmentally Friendly Building: New Seasons Market, Portland, Oregon

Brian Rohter is the CEO of New Seasons Market, a locally owned and operated group of grocery stores in Portland, Oregon. He was well into the development of the company's fifth store when a representative from the local neighborhood association approached him with an environmental concern—storm-water runoff.

Besides polluting rivers and streams, runoff after rain causes flooding and erosion, destroying habitats and contributing to sewer overflows. Plans for the latest New Seasons Market included adding 15,000 square feet of nonpermeable surfaces (surfaces covered by buildings or pavement) to the existing site, which would mean another one million gallons of storm water flowing out to the Willamette River.

Brian learned that Portland's Bureau of Environmental Services had grant money available for businesses interested in implementing storm-water controls. By creating "bioswales," marshy wetlands that absorb and filter runoff, around the new store, Brian could reduce the impact his building would have on the environment.

However, the project was already well underway and to make modifications would most likely mean increased costs and a delay in opening. Not only would Brian have to ask the architects for new drawings and apply for a grant to help cover the cost of building the bioswales, but he would have to obtain new permits from the city. Brian's experiences with the city so far had not always been smooth. The process of getting the original permits had been long, slow, and frustrating, and he was sure that the redesign would significantly postpone the store's opening.

But this was an opportunity that could not be missed; New Seasons wanted to be an environmental leader in the community and an inspiration to other businesses. With little deliberation, Brian decided to stop the building process, asked his architect for a redesign, and braced himself for yet another round of negotiations with the city.

His willingness to be flexible for the good of the community paid off. A local environmental organization volunteered to help New Seasons convene a working group, which included representatives from the neighborhood association, the Portland Bureau of Environmental Services, and the Portland Bureau of Development Services. Everyone was impressed with New Seasons' readiness to navigate the potential roadblocks associated with changing the building plans. With all of the entities at the table focused on issues of water quality, the group easily reached agreement on the need to amend the building plans in order to incorporate bioswales.

Much to Brian's surprise, once this common ground was established, things began happening quickly. New plans were drawn up and submitted, the city agreed to grant $50,000 for the bioswales, and the permit applications were hand-carried by city employees between departments to speed up the process. A few months later, the new store opened—on time.

The market's bioswales absorb over one million gallons of storm water annually, preventing water from becoming tainted and flowing into the Willamette River. New Seasons intends to include bioswales in the planning for future stores. The company is sharing its experience with other businesses and hopes many will follow its lead. By aligning its goal of being an environmental and community leader with an ecological need identified by the city, New Seasons developed an effective partnership with the local government. By finding common ground with the Bureau of Development Services, New Seasons produced a winning result for the company, the city, and the community and opened doors for other collaborative opportunities in the future.

Partnering with government agencies in one particular area or program can lead to other collaborations that benefit the community. The list of possible business-government collaborations is boundless, and once you begin the process, the waters feel a bit more friendly and you will begin to broaden your horizons. Cascade Engineering has spent years working with government agencies to train and hire people who were receiving government financial support and to move them off the welfare roll and onto the Cascade Engineering payroll.

Moving People off Welfare and into Jobs That Pay a Living Wage: Cascade Engineering, Grand Rapids, Michigan

Cascade Engineering, based in Grand Rapids, Michigan, is in the plastic injection molding business. It manufactures parts for the automotive and solid waste markets. Founded by Fred Keller in 1973, the Cascade Engineering Family of Companies has sales of over $280 million and employs 1,200 people (about half of whom are people of color).

Cascade is serious about its support for the community and issues an annual triple bottom line report that measures the company's financial, environmental, and social impact. In 1992 Fred and his manager of community partnerships and workforce diversity, Ron Jimmerson, created a program to transition people on welfare into full-time employment at Cascade. The Welfare to Work program began with twenty participants and high hopes. Although their intentions were good, Fred and Ron didn't have the necessary experience in this type of program.

When all of the participants dropped out, they realized they needed to start over again with something different.

The next effort was the Work to Work program. Cascade would hire employees who had worked for six months or more at a group of local Burger King restaurants. This program failed because few people worked at a Burger King for as long as six months because they couldn't live on the wages the restaurant chain paid its employees.

Not to be deterred, Fred and Ron started from scratch once again. This time they used a much different approach, and the third effort was a success. First of all, they decided to call the program Welfare to Career. This name change was important because it reflected a change in the content of the program and, equally important, it affected how the participants felt. It opened up opportunities for them and gave them hope.

Second, they sought the assistance of outside agencies so each organization could do what it did best. For example, they contracted with the Four C's Child Care to assist the participants in caring for their children, and the state Department of Human Services covered 80 percent of the cost. They also worked with Angel Wings, a Christian-based company staffed by highly trained drivers, to transport employees to work. For those with children, Cascade worked with the municipal transit system to pick up the parents and children together, drop off the children at day care, and then take the parents to Cascade. These and other partnerships made a huge impact on the participants and on their job attendance.

The third big difference in the Welfare to Career program was bringing in Ruby Payne, PhD, and her consulting firm. Her book, *A Framework for Understanding Poverty,* and training provided a major breakthrough for Cascade by providing a structure for the program. She taught Fred and Ron that every culture has different rules and norms of behavior and that moving people from welfare to financial independence requires a complete overhaul of their personal support system. In order for this program to succeed, it had to give participants what they needed to become a part of middle-class society, something Fred and Ron previously hadn't understood.

They now know that teaching new employees job skills isn't enough. These work-related competencies don't by themselves give employees the knowledge of how to manage money, hold down a job, and create a consistent and fulfilling life. As part of the program, Cascade began offering on-site personal and career development classes on topics such as money management.

Cascade partnered with the Inner City Christian Federation (ICCF) to prepare new employees for purchasing a home. ICCF specializes in building homes for low-income people in the inner city. It counsels these people in purchasing a home and learning how to manage their finances and maintain and care for their new home. In many cases Cascade's employees were paying more in rent than they would be paying for a home mortgage. Cascade also worked with Habitat for Humanity to connect participants with this nonprofit dedicated to increasing home ownership. To date, eight graduates of the Welfare to Career program have moved into Habitat for Humanity homes, and seven others have purchased homes with the help of other programs.

Cascade also helps guide the employees to other government agencies that can be of help. For example, a state of Michigan program helps qualified people purchase automobiles. So far, over sixty employees have bought cars through this program.

Each Welfare to Career participant begins work in a production capacity at a living wage of $9 per hour. Some have advanced to the point where they are earning $14.50 per hour. After a ninety-day probation period, staff members receive 100 percent of their health insurance benefits. They are also eligible for the company educational reimbursement of up to $2,000 per year for higher education classes that would help the company. The Welfare to Career program has grown to include a high of forty participants, and at one point over a hundred graduates of the Welfare to Career program were working at Cascade. Of the forty that went through the program in 2004–2005, thirty-eight no longer receive cash assistance from the government. By any measure this is a big success and a wonderful example of a program that includes not just one but multiple partnerships with government and nonprofit agencies for the extensive benefit of the community.

Building bridges with government agencies as a strategy for growing local value has been proven to work. Besides doing good for the community, these partnerships can give you a competitive advantage, enabling you to expand your business and increase your profitability.

Lessons Learned: Partnering with Government Agencies

Following are some of the lessons you may have gleaned from the examples given in this chapter:

- **Don't fight City Hall.** Don't rule out a government agency as a strategic partner for your business. Agencies may have relatively large budgets and substantial human resources, and they touch thousands of people's lives. Federal, state, and local governments often look to the private sector to partner on projects and programs for which they need expertise or a quick turnaround.
- **Learn the lingo and remember that patience is a virtue.** When choosing to work with government agencies, walk in with your eyes wide open about the challenges involved.

Study the system and talk with others who have had direct experience in order to identify "hot buttons" that the agency cares about. When you work with a government bureaucracy, every step generally takes longer—factor this into your business plan.

- **Be known as a bridge builder.** Networking and community involvement are essential for gaining traction in the public domain. Being known as a consensus-building community leader in your field can be a real asset when partnering with government agencies.

- **Work with government programs to meet hiring and training needs.** Many businesses are finding it difficult to find qualified employees, and in fact some are on a constant search to fill job vacancies. Effective government programs are available that can help you identify (and offer ongoing training and support to) unemployed or underemployed local residents who could become excellent staff members. Ultimately, business-government partnerships like these will play a critical role in ending poverty.

- **Go back to school.** Business and school partnerships have proven to be highly effective ways of improving local public education systems. Developing an ongoing business project that contributes to your local schools creates a strong connection to the community and is greatly appreciated by all your employees, especially those with school-age children.

8

Building a bridge
to the future

As an entrepreneur you can build a business that contributes to your community in ways that go far beyond selling a good product. You can leverage your relationships with all of your stakeholders to help strengthen your community and contribute to the common good.

This becomes even more profound when you consider that you are helping create a feeling of home and a sense of place for people in your community. Having a home is important to all of us. It may not be perfect, but when we think of home we want it to feel comfortable and safe and to bring warmth to our hearts.

Not everyone has a home. Even people who own a house may not feel secure or might even feel homeless. When we are physically or psychologically disconnected, we feel alienated from our world. We may have more technological conveniences today, but these devices don't help us feel grounded in a community.

Feeling at home comes from those invisible social, emotional, and spiritual parts of us that we experience through relationships with other people. When no one is around whom we know or love or can talk with, we feel isolated and not a part of a community. We may be surrounded by people and yet be lonely.

It's almost paradoxical that the invisible sensations that form the essence of feeling at home are often deeply connected to the structural spaces of our community. When our community is set up in a way that encourages connections through schools, houses of worship, shops, health clubs, cafes, and public spaces, we develop a sense of place; we feel more grounded and whole.

Feeling a sense of place is especially important for Americans because we are such a restless and transient bunch. Even though we highly value family, we'll never be tied down to a place strictly because our relatives and friends live there. Local businesses can play a vital role in making people feel at home and in creating a sense of community. Your business may already be a place that welcomes local residents and is deeply embedded in the culture of your community life, offering an important antidote to the malady of alienation.

Building a Legacy and a Source of Community Pride

Everyone wants to feel pride about the elements that make up his or her community. Living in Boston and not having Fenway Park and the Red Sox would make life in Boston feel sterile and the character of the city would be diminished. (Even if you've never been to Fenway, knowing it's there means something.) If you live in Wisconsin, you might say the same about life without the Green Bay Packers. And on a smaller scale we can all list local establishments that help give our communities character and charm. Your business may be the Red Sox of your community. Local businesses are key components of a vibrant and lively community life, and when they're good, they are worth preserving.

When you build your business, consider building a legacy as one of your goals. Establishing a successful business is no mean feat, and honoring its heritage is important. Putting your heart and soul into your company and then "cashing out" to a large corporation may be right for some entrepreneurs, but many other creative options are available for entrepreneurs who want to transition out of their companies. Because local businesses are having such a difficult time in today's business climate, the value of a business legacy to a community is even more profound.

Gun sold her business to a privately held company that has adopted and upheld the strongly held values that Gun and Tom Denhart instilled into the Hanna Andersson culture. Five years later, the values and social programs of Hanna are alive and kicking!

Laury's business is in its twenty-seventh year and going strong. He has witnessed many of his contemporaries sell to large corporate chains and has seen the negative results—club members receive poor service, staff members are unhappy, and the entrepreneur is wealthier but not feeling good about the sale. Laury's long-term objective is clear. He's developing a succession strategy for the Longfellow Clubs in order to keep the legacy of Longfellow alive for another thirty years and more.

Growing a business is all about building bridges with hundreds and even thousands of stakeholders. These trusty and well-worn bridges have great value and make a big difference in many lives. Be open to building a values-based legacy business that is in a constant process of reinventing and strengthening existing bridges while keeping an eye out for new and bold bridges to build. This rainbow of diverse connections is what creates a sense of place and makes us feel at home.

Joining Together to Build a Better Community
and a Better World

At a recent SVN conference and shortly thereafter at the International BALLE Conference in Burlington, Vermont, values-driven entrepreneurs gathered with leaders in the nonprofit and public sectors to share ideas and strategize on how business can build a sustainable and strong economy. In a spirited and sometimes emotional conversation, participants engaged with Seventh Generation's Jeff Hollender and Wild Planet Toys' Jennifer Chapman after they presented their differing perspectives on doing business with Wal-Mart to over 200 entrepreneurs and other business leaders. After a healthy lunch sourced primarily from local organic farms, Judy Wicks of the White Dog Cafe joined with farmers, restaurant owners, and other community leaders in a healthy dialogue on how to build strong local food systems. Ed Dugger of UNC Partners and Glynn Lloyd of City Fresh Foods met with leaders from several business-related nonprofits to talk about how to effectively support the growth and development of businesses owned by people of color. Tom and Kate Chappell eloquently shared their very cogent and yet controversial case for why they sold their more than thirty-year-old business to the giant corporation Colgate-Palmolive. Mal Warwick, the chair of SVN, introduced the initial installment of this SVN book series, which for the first time offers entrepreneurs strategies and hands-on advice on how to build businesses that can help change the world. Imagine yourself involved in one of these highly energized gatherings of like-minded visionaries working for a common purpose. Then don't just imagine it; join us in this good work.

Over the next thirty years, through conversations like these, entrepreneurs like you can help transform the world of commerce so that human values lead business growth, not only the drive for higher profits. We invite you to join thousands of others in this mission to grow local value and build a just and sustainable world.

Love

Finally, we hope you are inspired to grow your local values-driven business and that you sense the love we have for the people involved in our businesses.

We talk openly about loving our jobs, loving life, and loving people. And we encourage others to do the same. In Gun's entrepreneurial years she often shared the following: "Apply love and respect in all you do. Love for your work, respect for others. It works wonders!" And the fading cut-up calendar slipped under the plastic cover of Laury's organizing binder summarizes his view on love: "Where love reigns the impossible is attained."

Notes

1. Civic Economics, Andersonville Development Corporation, and the Andersonville Chamber of Commerce, *The Andersonville Study of Retail Economics,* October 2004, Business Alliance for Local Living Economies, http://www.livingeconomies.org/localfirst/studies/index_html#9 (accessed July 12, 2006).
2. Honda of America Mfg., Inc., "Honda in Ohio: Economic Multiplier Effects," http://www.ohio.honda.com/Ohio/Multiplier.cfm (accessed July 12, 2006).
3. Betsy Burton, *The King's English: Adventures of an Independent Bookseller* (Salt Lake City: Gibbs Smith, 2005).
4. Ewing Marion Kauffman Foundation, *Women and Angel Investing: An Untapped Pool of Equity for Entrepreneurs,* April 27, 2006, http://www.kauffman.org/items.cfm?itemID=699 (accessed July 12, 2006).
5. Manjari Raman, "Economic Justice," (PowerPoint presentation, Social Venture Network Conference, Kennebunkport, ME, April 21, 2006.)
6. Leigh Buchanan, "The 2006 Inner City 100," *Inc.,* June 2006, http://www.inc.com/magazine/20060601/ic100-91-100.html (accessed July 12, 2006).
7. Bo Burlingham, "The Coolest Small Company in America," *Inc.,* January 2003, http://www.inc.com/magazine/20030101/25036.html (accessed July 12, 2006).
8. John Abrams, *The Company We Keep: Reinventing Small Business for People, Community, and Place* (White River Junction, VT: Chelsea Green Publishing Company, 2005).
9. Susan Dewhirst (media relations manager) and Rob Robinson (partnership leader), Tom's of Maine, interview by Gun Denhart, Kennebunk, ME, November 21, 2005.
10. Ibid.
11. Paul Hawken, *The Ecology of Commerce* (New York: Harper-Collins Publishers, 1993).

12. Paul Hawken, Amory Lovins, and L. Hunter Lovins, *Natural Capitalism: Creating the Next Industrial Revolution* (Boston: Little, Brown and Company, 1999), 2.
13. Dave Mezzacappa, "Reading Program Gets Rave Reviews," *Philadelphia Inquirer,* November 24, 1997.

Suggested Reading

John Abrams. *The Company We Keep: Reinventing Small Business for People, Community, and Place.* White River Junction, VT: Chelsea Green Publishing Company, 2005.

Mark Albion. *Leading a Values-Based Business.* San Francisco: Berrett-Koehler Publishers, 2006.

Bo Burlingham. *Small Giants: Companies That Choose to Be Great Instead of Big.* New York: Portfolio, 2005.

Betsy Burton. *The King's English: Adventures of an Independent Bookseller.* Salt Lake City: Gibbs Smith, Publisher, 2005.

Ben Cohen and Jerry Greenfield. *Ben and Jerry's Double-Dip: How to Run a Values-Led Business and Make Money, Too!* New York: Simon and Schuster Paperbacks, 1997.

Ben Cohen and Mal Warwick. *Values-Driven Business: How to Change the World, Make Money, and Have Fun.* San Francisco: Berrett-Koehler Publishers, 2006.

Paul Hawken. *The Ecology of Commerce.* New York: HarperCollins Publishers, 1993.

Paul Hawken, Amory Lovins, and L. Hunter Lovins. *Natural Capitalism: Creating the Next Industrial Revolution.* Boston: Little, Brown and Company, 1999.

Jeffrey Hollender. *What Matters Most: How a Small Group of Pioneers Is Teaching Social Responsibility to Big Business, and Why Big Business Is Listening.* New York: Basic Books, 2004.

David Korten. *The Great Turning: From Empire to Earth Community.* San Francisco: Berrett-Koehler Publishers, 2006.

David Korten. *When Corporations Rule the World.* Bloomfield, CT: Kumana Press, 2001.

John Robbins. *The Food Revolution: How Your Diet Can Help Save Your Life and the World.* Berkeley, CA: Conari Press, 2001.

Michael Shuman. *Going Local: Creating Self-Reliant Communities in a Global Age.* New York: Routledge, 2000.

Michael Shuman. *The Small-Mart Revolution: How Local Businesses Are Beating the Global Competition.* San Francisco: Berrett-Koehler Publishers, 2006.

Resources

Following is a list of Web sites you can visit and organizations you can contact to find information that will help you grow local value.

The American Reading Company
http://www.100bookchallenge.com
Bazzani Associates
http://www.bazzani.com
Bright Horizons Family Solutions
http://www.brighthorizons.com
Business Alliance for Local Living Economies
http:www.livingeconomies.org
Cascade Engineering
http://www.cascadeng.com
City Fresh Foods
http://www.cityfreshfoods.com
Gardener's Supply
http://www.gardeners.com
Greyston Bakery
http://www.greystonbakery.com
Hanna Andersson
http://www.hannaandersson.com
Higgins Restaurant
http://higgins.citysearch.com
Horizons for Homeless Children
http://www.horizonsinitiative.org
Initiative for a Competitive Inner City
http:www.icic.org
Intervale Center
http:www.intervale.org
Investors' Circle
http:/www.investorscircle.net

Joie de Vivre Hospitality
http://www.jdvhospitality.com
The King's English Book Shop
http://www.kingsenglish.com
The Longfellow Clubs
http://www.longfellowclubs.com
New Seasons Market
http://www.newseasonsmarket.com
Powell's Books
http://www.powells.com
Rejuvenation
http://www.rejuvenation.com
Roxbury Technology Corporation
http://www.roxburytechnology.com
Seven Stars Organic Yogurt
http://www.sevenstarsfarm.com
Small Potatoes Urban Delivery
https://www.spud.ca
Social Venture Network
http://www.svn.org
South Mountain Company
http://www.somoco.com
TAGS Hardware
http://www.tagshardware.com
Tom's of Maine
http://www.tomsofmaine.com
White Dog Cafe
http://www.whitedog.com
Wild Planet Toys
http://www.wildplanet.com
Zingerman's Delicatessen
http://www.zingermans.com

Index

About Social Venture Network

SVN transforms the way the world does business by connecting, leveraging, and promoting a global community of leaders for a more just and sustainable economy.

Since its founding in 1987, SVN has grown from a handful of visionary individuals into a vibrant community of 400 business owners, investors, and nonprofit leaders who are advancing the movement for social responsibility in business. SVN members believe in a new bottom line for business, one that values healthy communities and the human spirit as well as high returns.

As a network, SVN facilitates partnerships, strategic alliances, and other ventures that promote social and economic justice. SVN compiles and promotes best practices for socially responsible enterprises and produces unique conferences that support the professional and personal development of business leaders and social entrepreneurs.

Please visit http://www.svn.org for more information on SVN membership, initiatives, and events.

About the Authors

In 1980 **Laury Hammel** founded The Longfellow Clubs, a group of health, tennis, and sports clubs located outside Boston and servicing over 10,000 members. The Longfellow Clubs has been a leader in the fitness and tennis industries and has won numerous awards. Laury has been inducted into the New England Tennis Hall of Fame, and his emphasis on growing local value has led *Club Business International* magazine to call him the "conscience of the industry." His family was named the National Tennis Family of the Year in 2000, and he is currently the number one tennis player in New England in his age group.

Laury has been a leader in the world of socially responsible business for over twenty years. He founded the first business association of socially responsible businesses in 1988—New England Business Association for Social Responsibility. Since then he has founded several other associations promoting socially responsible business, including Business for Social Responsibility (BSR) and the International Symposium for Spirituality and Business held at Babson College. In 2001, with Judy Wicks, he cofounded the Business Alliance for Local Living Economies (BALLE). As its cochair he enjoys traveling around North America planting seeds that sprout into local BALLE networks.

Gun Denhart cofounded the Hanna Andersson children's clothing company in 1983. Through her leadership, the company has become known for its high-quality clothing made from soft cotton materials as well as community involvement and family-friendly work practices.

The company has received numerous recognitions, including the Business Enterprise Trust award and Direct Mail Marketing Association's Catalog of the Year award. *Working Woman* magazine has recognized Hanna in its annual list of 100 Best Companies for Working Mothers for company policies such as flextime and child-care reimbursement.

Her company gave 5 percent of its pretax profits to groups advocating and providing for children. In 2001 when the company was sold, Gun founded Hanna Andersson Children's Foundation, which promotes a brighter future for vulnerable children. Funds are allocated by employees to support programs in the communities where Hanna and its vendors have a presence. Gun chairs the nonprofit Stand for Children, a national grass-roots group advocating for children.

Hanna Andersson was a charter member of the national organization Business for Social Responsibility. It was also a founding member of the Oregon Business Association, a progressive group that works on finding common ground on statewide public policy issues.

Other Titles in the
Social Venture Network Series

Values-Driven Business: How to Change the World,
Make Money, and Have Fun
by Ben Cohen and Mal Warwick
This short, easy-to-read book details every step in the process of
creating and managing a small or midsized business that will reflect your personal values, not force you to hide them. As cofounder of the immensely successful Ben & Jerry's Homemade Ice
Cream, Ben Cohen is one of the best-known examples of personal
integrity and social commitment in the business community. Social Venture Network chair Mal Warwick is the leader of one of
the world's most respected organizations committed to building a
just and sustainable world through business. They show how vir-
tually any small business can be efficient, competitive, and successful while pursuing a "triple bottom line" of profit, people, and
planet.
*February 2006, $12.00, paperback. ISBN 978-1-57675-358-3 or
1-57675-358-1*

True to Yourself: Leading a Values-Based Business
by Mark Albion
This is an engaging, accessible guide to a critical component of
socially responsible business: effective leadership. Mark Albion,
author of the *New York Times* bestseller *Making a Life, Making a Living,* argues that small-business leaders concerned with
more than the bottom line are not only more fulfilled but also
more successful with more sustainable lives. Whether you're just
starting out or many years on your way, *True to Yourself* will
help you to get and stay on track.
*July 2006, $12.00, paperback, ISBN 978-1-57675-378-1 or
1-57675-378-6*

Marketing That Matters: 10 Practices to Drive
Your Socially Responsible Business
by Chip Conley and Eric Friedenwald-Fishman
"Marketing" is not a dirty word or a last resort—it is key to advancing the mission of any socially responsible business. Award-winning marketers Chip Conley and Eric Friedenwald-Fishman offer values-driven businesspeople an in-the-trenches guide to building effective marketing models for their companies. They provide practical steps for incorporating marketing as a core element of the business. Full of inspiring stories and tested advice, this book shows how to sell what you do without selling your soul.
October 2006, $12.00, paperback, ISBN 978-1-57675-383-5 or 1-57675-383-2

Values Sell: Transforming Purpose into Profit Through
Creative Sales and Distribution Strategies
by Nadine A. Thompson and Angela E. Soper
In this practical and inspiring guide, Nadine Thompson and Angela Soper draw on real-world examples to show how a values-driven business can establish a foundation from which innovative sales and distribution strategies naturally flow. They lay out concrete steps for communicating a powerful, motivating vision for the business and for designing sales and distribution strategies that fit the needs, interests, and habits of your target customer.
February 2007, $12.00, paperback, ISBN 978-1-57675-421-4 or 1-57675-421-9

For more information, check out the
Social Venture Network series Web page:
www.svnbooks.com.

About Berrett-Koehler Publishers

Berrett-Koehler is an independent publisher dedicated to an ambitious mission: Creating a World That Works for All.

We believe that to truly create a better world, action is needed at all levels—individual, organizational, and societal. At the individual level, our publications help people align their lives with their values and with their aspirations for a better world. At the organizational level, our publications promote progressive leadership and management practices, socially responsible approaches to business, and humane and effective organizations. At the societal level, our publications advance social and economic justice, shared prosperity, sustainability, and new solutions to national and global issues.

A major theme of our publications is "Opening Up New Space." They challenge conventional thinking, introduce new ideas, and foster positive change. Their common quest is changing the underlying beliefs, mind-sets, institutions, and structures that keep generating the same cycles of problems, no matter who our leaders are or what improvement programs we adopt.

We strive to practice what we preach—to operate our publishing company in line with the ideas in our books. At the core of our approach is *stewardship,* which we define as a deep sense of responsibility to administer the company for the benefit of all of our "stakeholder" groups: authors, customers, employees, investors, service providers, and the communities and environment around us.

We are grateful to the thousands of readers, authors, and other friends of the company who consider themselves to be part of the "BK Community." We hope that you, too, will join us in our mission.

Be Connected

Visit Our Website

Go to www.bkconnection.com to read exclusive previews and excerpts of new books, find detailed information on all Berrett-Koehler titles and authors, browse subject-area libraries of books, and get special discounts.

Subscribe to Our Free E-Newsletter

Be the first to hear about new publications, special discount offers, exclusive articles, news about bestsellers, and more! Get on the list for our free e-newsletter by going to www.bkconnection.com.

Participate in the Discussion

To see what others are saying about our books and post your own thoughts, check out our blogs at www.bkblogs.com.

Get Quantity Discounts

Berrett-Koehler books are available at quantity discounts for orders of ten or more copies. Please call us toll-free at (800) 929-2929 or email us at bkp.orders@aidcvt.com.

Host a Reading Group

For tips on how to form and carry on a book reading group in your workplace or community, see our website at www.bkconnection.com.

Join the BK Community

Thousands of readers of our books have become part of the "BK Community" by participating in events featuring our authors, reviewing draft manuscripts of forthcoming books, spreading the word about their favorite books, and supporting our publishing program in other ways. If you would like to join the BK Community, please contact us at bkcommunity@bkpub.com.